Child of
The Diaspora

Michael A. Hutchinson

Shield  Crest

ISBN: 978-1-910176-64-1

MMXV

Published by
ShieldCrest
Aylesbury, Buckinghamshire, HP22 5RR
England
www.shieldcrest.co.uk

DEDICATION

This book is dedicated to my wife Lynne, my brother John, my cousin Stan and his wife Anne and to the memory of my late mum and dad. Sadly, neither my brother nor I were ever able to know any relations on our mum's side, because their untimely deaths were to occur not much more than a year before my brother John was born.

My wife Lynne has given me unflinching patience, support and encouragement throughout, despite the protracted preparation of this book – for which I take full responsibility - and for that support I am forever grateful! Furthermore, both Stan and Anne have willingly and generously given of their time in helping me to put my parents' early lives as a couple into some kind of context, albeit brief at this point in time. My older brother John has kindly drawn upon his memories of childhood and youth to fill-in the gaps in mine in this respect.

It is my avowed intention to provide a fuller picture of my late dad's life in the planned sequel to this book, and so do fuller justice to the memory of my late dad and to the research work undertaken over a good many years by my cousins on my late dad's side of the family.

Finally I wish to dedicate this book to all who died during the Second World War, especially my late mum's co-patriots, and to the hope that succeeding generations will never forget what happened to them.

ACKNOWLEDGMENTS

I am indebted to a whole group of people, both individuals and those attached to organisations, in the UK and overseas, who have provided me with a fantastic amount of help over a period of more than two decades whilst I have been assiduously learning about recent European history and constructing my family-tree. Whilst I will be the first to admit that the verdict, in both instances, is 'work in progress', I would never have 'got off the starting-blocks' with this book without the unsparing and patient support of these kind people. In particular, I wish to mention staff at IKG Wien/Vienna [Israelitische Kultusgemeinde Wien], at DÖW Wien/Vienna [Dokumentationsarchiv des Österreichischen Widerstandes], and the Austrian National Archives in Vienna. I also owe a debt of gratitude to Mrs Joan Adler at the *Gesher Galicia* genealogy database organisation based in the United States, who has always given of her very valuable time in answering my family tree queries over the years.

I wish to acknowledge in particular the knowledge I have gained through studying the published research work undertaken by numerous writers on the history of the Holocaust, especially the series of books written by the late Sir Martin Gilbert. Furthermore I am grateful for the kindness shown by staff at the Association of Jewish Refugees in London and by present-day residents [including Marguerite] in Church Lane, Ufford, near Woodbridge, Suffolk, UK, where I grew up and spent many enjoyable years in my childhood and youth.

Last but not least, I wish to thank Mike Ptycia, a good friend of ours, without whose IT skills the book would never have reached print. So, thank you Mike!

CONTENTS

PREFACE

When Bob, the lorry driver for the firm that I worked for, asked me 'out of the blue' whether I was Jewish, I said, albeit hesitantly, "No, but why?" To which he replied with words to the effect: "I was just wondering!" It didn't seem the sort of question that an employee of a firm would normally ask another in the course of passing them by in the works yard, office or whatever, so maybe curiosity got the better of him that morning, when we passed in the nursery yard.

No more was subsequently said on the matter, but it got me thinking. Being named Michael, and thinking at the time that maybe I did have a Jewish face, were two reasonable prompts for his question, though the notion that I may have inherited Jewish mannerisms from my mother did not enter my head at the time. And mum had maybe been rather economic with the truth when she had explained to my brother and I that we had been circumcised as babies for medical hygiene reasons! Besides which, I had no idea at the time that male circumcision was so crucial to Jewish identity from way back to the Israelites, centuries before the birth of Jesus Christ. That apart, when and where was I circumcised? And would that have been the age when Jewish boys from time immemorial would have been circumcised? And would they, for example, have carried out such procedures at the Ipswich general hospital, being the hospital closest to my home when I was a baby and where I grew up? Strange questions, you might say, for me to ask as a virtual septuagenarian!

Fast forward thirty five or so years from Bob's question, and ask me about family resemblances, and I would answer differently. For now, thanks to my paternal cousins, I have a copy of a photo of my Geordie grandma on my dad's side of the family, and I would more likely say that I bore a stronger resemblance to her than to my late mother. In short, I am on a journey to discover my true identity, a journey of exploration which began in earnest when my late mother died, and which, sometimes frustratingly, has seemed to raise more questions than answers. Readers must judge from the picture of my late dad's mum on the front cover of the book!

This book is about a journey which is ongoing, and about circumstances and events which have thus far been its building blocks. The period covered by this book has witnessed some momentous events on the British, European and World stage, and I have tried to piece together my family's life and the way that these events have impinged on it. I aim to offer a personal perspective on family-life in England from the onset of the Second World War. In so doing, and because many of the events took place before I was born, I have necessarily attempted to provide a personal interpretation of other peoples' accounts, especially in relation to some of the momentous and indescribable events that have besmirched recent European-, not to say world-history. Shortcomings are therefore my responsibility.

I set out initially to chronicle the lives of my late mother and father in tandem, whilst describing how my brother and I figured in their lives and subsequently on our own. The aim, within a single volume, was to place my parents' lives and our growing up in the wider context of a period in the history of Britain and the modern world that will never be forgotten. As my journey has progressed I have come to realise that I faced two very different and not easily reconcilable tasks. Unravelling my late mother's life, even when some evidence proved to be sketchy if not non-existent, needed to be separate from the imperfect records and memories relating to my late dad. Such was the extremely limited contact that my brother and I had with dad's side of the family during our formative years - and indeed for decades after - that I seemed to be starting virtually from square one. Even though my dad was my very own biological dad and was one of my next-of-kin for so many years, my `separation' from him and his side of the family – for reasons that I'm still pondering over - led me to liken my task to that of the occasional guest in the British Broadcasting Corporation [BBC]'s television series `Who Do You Think You Are?' who starts with a virtually blank canvas and has to search high and low to begin to appreciate the lives of his or her hitherto unknown ancestors. I needed to learn about paternal ancestors who, for one reason or another, had hitherto been largely unknown to me. I would not have done justice to my late father or to my cousins on his side of my family if I had attempted to combine his side of the story with that of my late mother, genealogically-imperfect and thin though it may be. This is why I have decided to make dad the subject of a follow-up volume. I could have employed a professional genealogist to undertake research, as is the case on the TV series, but I would not have been able to afford it and, besides which, it would have taken away the challenges that confront an amateur [novice] Brit embarking upon Central-and Eastern European genealogy.

My present account is inevitably a very personal – and sometimes anecdotal - view that draws heavily on my own recollection of people and events that I came to know and experience first-hand, supported by what I hope is a reasonably objective perspective of pan-European historical events and events that have affected my own life. Lots of us with some personal connection to epic present-day power-struggles, such as that presently unfolding in my late `granddad's' Ukraine, come to set these within the framework of their own `take' on recent history, shaped maybe by this personal/family connection with the nations and citizens involved. My story represents just such a personal viewpoint, enriching my perception of my own identity in the process. I am acutely aware that I have not discussed the utter depravity in Cambodia, Vietnam or in Bosnia, Serbia and

Herzegovina. I can only say that the loss of life and the indifference to it shown by the perpetrators is, regrettably, a further demonstration of how low we can reach as people. More importantly, however, it is all the more reason why we need to address it meaningfully at grass-roots level as well as on the world-stage. Too often it is individuals who opt to perpetrate wrongs against society in the hope that accountability – if it was ever able to lift the heads of victims above water-level - can only stop with organisations to which wrongdoers may or may not belong; I think the legal notion is `vicarious liability'. Some would indeed beg to disagree about where the buck should stop.

1 JOURNEY'S BEGINNING

As a young teenager, I distinctly remember an anthology of essays [but not its title!] on the Second World War which had been published in the United States in the 1950s, the gist of one of them being that Adolf Hitler was insane. We had been given the book by an American Air Force family moving out of their rented cottage near the Bradleys and Orfords in Ufford. This essay has stuck in my mind ever since I read it, though at that time I had no idea of the profound personal significance of what I was reading. So has the poetry from World War One written by Wilfred Owen, Siegfried Sassoon and others. But Hitler needed his wider sympathisers' and collaborators' support, including not only many Germans and Austrians, but that of the ruling Japanese of the time, Mussolini in Italy and the Vichy régime in France. I ponder on that when digesting Carl Jung's remarks. In a BBC radio broadcast in 1946, psychologist Carl Jung reflected:

"The fact that one member of the European family [I.e. Germany] could sink to the level of the concentration camp throws a dubious light on all the others. Who are we to imagine that 'it couldn't happen here'? [...] "......a terrible doubt about humanity, and about ourselves, gnaws at our heart...[yet] such a state of degradation can come about only under certain conditions. The most important of these is the accumulation of urban, industrialized masses- of people torn from the soil, engaged in one-sided employment, and lacking every healthy instinct, even that of self-preservation... Loss of the instinct of self-preservation can be measured in terms of dependence on the state.... [which] means that everybody relies on everybody else (=State) instead of on himself..... for

1

one is still hanging in the air even when hanging in the company of ten thousand other people. The only difference is that one is no longer aware of one's own insecurity..... The steady growth of the Welfare State is no doubt a very fine thing from one point of view, but from another it is a doubtful blessing, as it robs people of their individual responsibility and turns them into infants and sheep. [...] ...once a man is cut off from the nourishing roots of instinct, he becomes the shuttle-cock of every wind that blows. He is then no better than a sick animal, demoralized and degenerate, and nothing short of a catastrophe can bring him back to health..... The increasing dependence on the State is anything but a healthy symptom; it means that the whole nation is in a fair way to becoming a herd of sheep, constantly relying on a shepherd to drive them into good pastures. This is a pathological, demoralized, and mentally abnormal condition: one side of us does things which the other (so called decent) side prefers to ignore.... Every man hangs on to the next and enjoys a false feeling of security,..] . In reality the chief accuser is not outside, but [is] the judge who dwells in our own hearts.....Since this is nature's attempt to bring about a cure, it would be wiser not to persist too long in rubbing the noses of Germans in their own abominations, lest we drown the voice of the accuser in their hearts... . [...]......The Germans were never wholly indifferent to the impression they made on the outside world. They resented disapproval and hated even to be criticized. Inferiority feelings make people touchy and lead to compensatory efforts to impress. As a result [...] 'German efficiency' is demonstrated with such aplomb that it leads to a reign of terror and the shooting of hostages. The German no longer thinks of these things as murder, for he is lost in considerations of his own prestige."

To say that my parents were traumatized by the Second World War and its personal impact is an understatement by any stretch of the imagination. And, for my dad's part, his upbringing was far from ideal. Thus, bringing up a young family in the aftermath of these circumstances was a doubly tall order that, in my view, neither of my parents was adequately prepared for. Perhaps for that reason, neither of them discussed their experiences with John or me, and only snippets of information were gleaned from books and magazines that found their way into our cottage-home. Not that this would have been unusual, for a good number of people whose grandfathers had died or had been seriously injured during the First World War have said that these ancestors could not bring themselves around to even talking about what had happened to them and their compatriots on the front-line. We boys were banned from speaking to my dad when he returned home for short stays in the 1960s, and this did not help matters either. I had no idea about his childhood until I spoke to my cousin Stan after dad's passing, but plan to elaborate on this in the follow-up to this book.

Trauma is a condition which would likely be recognised in different ways by the layperson and the specialist. The layperson will have seen the symptoms but won't necessarily have associated them with an underlying cause. Perhaps for that reason, neither mum nor dad discussed their wartime experiences with John or me. It is only in hindsight that we are beginning to understand the mental effects on soldiers and civilians alike of atrocities they have witnessed at first-hand on the front line in the First and Second World Wars, the Korean and Vietnam Wars, the Cambodian tragedy, as well as what has been taking place more recently in Central Europe, the Balkans, Syria, Palestine, Afghanistan and Iraq. Likewise, to escape from atrocities of unbelievable barbarity and then to hear years later that your mother and brother were victims of that very barbarity, cannot fail but leave an indelible mark on anyone's soul and psyche, and therefore their ongoing behaviour, sense of trust and security and attitudes toward other people. There seem to be worrying undertones of this which underlay my late mother's behaviour later in her life, and I hope to return to this notion in the proposed sequel to this book.

Basically, my parents had no support-system when they brought John and me into this world. Dad had been orphaned as a child, and, as for my mother's family, I guess that I drew a blank. We did not know what having grandparents meant, so we did not miss them, especially as we grew up. Nevertheless, both John and I were fortunate in being able to benefit from the support given by our mother and our friends' parents in our village of Ufford. I mention the Millers, but there were also the Turners in neighbouring Bromeswell. Richard Turner was John's class-mate at Secondary High School and his father ran a rubbish disposal business that included the nearby USAF airbase as one if its customers. I seem to recollect that Richard's father owned a large American Cadillac type of car, and that John used to cycle over to Richard's house to join in with family-life there. Occasionally I would be invited over, and joined Richard's younger brother Barry out and about on our bikes near their home, or watching TV. `Telly' was a novel thing in the later fifties, so John and I were quite `privileged' in that sense. Mum was quite happy for us to spend free-time with our friends, and she would be content knitting or darning, preparing food or listening to our valve-radio which cost us four shillings a quarter [or it may have been a year!] to hire from Radio Rentals, and sat squarely on top of the kitchen dresser in `dad's' corner of the kitchen. There came a time when the rental company no longer deemed it worthwhile to maintain the service contract, so gave the radio to us. It remained in good working order for years to come.

The valve radio was a kind of lifeline for all of us. When we were young, it was *Children's Hour* that entertained John and I, whilst my parents preferred the 6 o'clock news on the Home Service. After dad went away to work, mum and we two boys huddled around the radio to listen to Radio Luxembourg, on wavelength 208. Our favourite programme was `*Take your Pick*,' featuring Wilfred and Mabel Pickles, though we were `addicted' to nightly episodes of *The Archers* on BBC radio. On Saturday evenings during the football season, John and I listened religiously to Sports Report with Eamon Andrews on the Light Programme, and we would all tune in to "*In Town Tonight*" later on in the evening on the same radio channel, to hear which famous people were passing through London. Sir Matt Busby was a guest on the programme on more than one occasion.

As teenagers, a rare treat was for John and I was to be allowed to take a train to Old Trafford, Manchester, to watch a big soccer game. We would already have sent off for tickets many weeks in advance, enclosing a postal order, which was the accepted method of money transfer in those days. And whilst we could catch the train via Sheffield to get to the match for a 3pm kick-off, our journey home to Suffolk had to be via a night's sleep-over in one of London's youth hostels. This was because there simply weren't any trains which ran from Manchester, via Sheffield, to Ipswich at the end of the match on Saturday evening. But it was all worth it when you were actually in the stadium watching Jimmy Greaves and Bobby Charlton score hat tricks in the same match. In those First Division football league days, all matches started at 3pm on Saturday afternoons and TV was not part of the professional football scene other than for the FA Cup Final. Our Old Trafford tickets would be for allocated seats, which, in retrospect, was amazing, given that we certainly couldn't buy tickets as easily as that today, even though the ground capacity has increased from 62,000 or so people [seats and terrace-standing] to just over 75,000 in the all-seater stadium today. And to be able to get the autographs of all the Chelsea players and Ted Drake the Manager on the train down to London after the match, was an added bonus for us!

When John was younger, he loved reading Enid Blyton's adventure stories, and would pass the books on to me to read. We kept them on the dressing table which mum had left in [what came to be] our bedroom, whilst the shelf behind my pillow boasted large colour photos of my favourite footballers gleaned from *"Charlie Buchan's Football Monthly"*, and proudly framed. These players were my heroes, and I tried to emulate them. And each year, mum would buy me a copy of David Jack's football statistics book, a very small but fat volume packed with data vital to any real football follower of the day!

Mum was a competent pianist, and quite early on she had acquired a second-hand piano which sat below the bay-window that overlooked Mrs. Morris's garden. Mum had also arranged for both John and I to have piano lessons on Thursday evenings after school. It was when we had parked our bicycles and walked into Mrs. Rowland's house on St John's Street, Woodbridge on February 6th, 1958 that we heard about the Munich air-crash on her radio, when, after a refuelling stop on its planned flight from Belgrade to Manchester, British European Airways flight 609 crashed on its third attempt to take off from a slush-covered runway. By 1958 I was more enthusiastic about playing football than playing the piano, although I cannot speak for my older brother John. Anyway, not by that time having a newspaper delivery job after school and conscious that it was not fair for mum to pay for lessons that we did not sufficiently value, we gave up our piano lessons.

In retrospect, I recognise that I had been most unappreciative, and that, with a good deal more application, I would have been able to go beyond a grasp of the rudimentary keyboard scales. After all, waltzes came naturally to our mum, who would love to hum away merrily when she heard the orchestral rendition of Strauss's "Blue Danube" on the radio. John was more dedicated than I in later life, and he was later to learn to play the violin and the flute.

As a family, we were not regular theatre-goers, but mum did take us to the pantomime at the Ipswich Repertory Theatre around Christmas time when we were younger, and would probably have invited our young village friends to join us. Mum and I did not discuss politics at home when I was a teenager, and, anyhow, chose to expend her energies on matters which she could influence in a meaningful way. Hence her enjoyment working with the local Brownies pack and with other women in the village Women's Institute. Mum had a selection of *Kilner* jars in the cold larder, and would preserve blackberries that we picked along the village hedgerows, as well as plums that we picked in the orchard at the top end of the village. We did not have television at home throughout the whole of my childhood, having grown up at the time when TV was only just emerging as an up-and-coming broadcasting medium. TVs were akin to cars at the time, in that they were classed as a luxury rather than as a necessity. And when I was working in London, John and dad did not have TV at home in Ufford, but mum and I did occasionally watch TV in the later 1960s when our digs were in a hotel in Bloomsbury. But we did not have a TV in our flat in West London from the late 1970s, and we did not buy newspapers regularly. Contrast this with our life earlier in Ufford, where mum used to read the *News Chronicle* which was delivered during the week and have the Sunday Times delivered by Jane Woodhouse's father, Reg. Furthermore, we all listened in to the BBC 6 o'clock news on the Home Service every evening, as well as our favourites on the BBC Light Programme and on Radio Luxembourg. It was around the time that the *Sunday Times* was bought up by Charles [Lord] Thompson and underwent a significant change in editorial content, that Mum stopped reading it. Besides which, this Sunday paper was becoming increasingly expensive and heavier by the week with colour supplements. And Friday night was Fish and Chips night in the lower village, when the fish and chips van stopped on the Knoll at the top of Church Lane, where we lived, and villagers queued up to buy a hearty fish meal, well wrapped in newspaper sheets. The van had its distinctive metal chimney and cowl, which became blackened over the years but was a welcome sight, especially on a cold winter's evening.

2 GROWING UP IN UFFORD, WOODBRIDGE AND IPSWICH

Our semi-detached cottage in Church Lane, Ufford, near Woodbridge, had been rented to us since the summer of 1945, shortly after I had been born. The empty cottage had been a tied estate cottage for workers on the Blois Brooke manor, one of six manors that existed at one time in Ufford, but all of which have now disappeared. And the manor house, together with all its trappings such as the sunken garden, the croquet lawn and summer house and the grand brick-wall flanked entrance drive gates at the top of our lane have left a lasting impression in my mind even though, the entrance gates apart, they have long since gone. That said, much of the honeycomb brick-wall that flanked the gates has been whisked away some years ago, maybe for reasons to do with vehicle-sightlines, so the drastically cut-back walls, along with the gates hung to them, sadly bring to mind false-pockets in a jacket!

The last remaining Ufford manor, Ufford Place, was sold upon the death in 1956 of Major Eardley Blois Brooke and then later destroyed in a fire. Fortunately the gates and piers survived; so our cottage had been built for agricultural workers and their families, who were employed on the Blois Brooke Estate, but these workers strove to protect their interests from quite early on. Friendly Societies and benefit clubs had existed since the late seventeenth century and during the last forty years of the eighteenth century their numbers increased significantly. It has been suggested that these were often 'front' organisations for unionised labour, illegal until 1799. By this point in time, roughly two out of three communities had at least one Friendly Society, providing healthcare and insurance, though their distribution was uneven and differed between urban and rural parishes. By 1804, Suffolk as a whole had over 300 such societies, and their 12,000 or so members constituted the seventh highest membership in the country, due largely to losing staple industries like wool. Of these more than half were in villages, partly through little demand from townsfolk and partly because local landowners and worthies promoted them.

The French ' Blois' in the Blois Brooke hints at the origins of this family, which I hazard to suggest goes back to the Norman Conquest and the distribution of estates across the country to his loyal friends by the William, the new French king of England. So what about the periods either side of the Norman Invasion of 1066? And what about the middle ages, the Renaissance, the nineteenth century and then the twentieth centuries? And where does Ufford come into all of this?

We know from the published history of Ufford's origins that in the 5th century, Anglo Saxons began to invade East Anglia and the Suffolk coast became a separate kingdom with the Wuffingas being the ruling family. The family gave its name to the village and thus we can account for the beginnings of Ufford, a ford with a hard gravel bed over the River Deben, crossing the narrow neck of marsh and river between the higher ground of Bromeswell and Ufford. Over the years the name has changed from *Juffeforda, Offewarda, Uffewarda, Ufforda, Usford* and finally to **Ufford**. We know that Saxon burials with weapons and ornaments were found in Ufford Place [the Blois Brooke's home] in 1819. We also know that the wealthy villages and the associated grand churches of West Suffolk, such as Lavenham, south-west of Ipswich, were built on the fortunes of the medieval wool industry in that area. But what about Ufford? Or Wickham Market? Or Woodbridge? Ufford church has one of the most elaborate font-covers in the country, and the size of the church together with its construction of knapped flints walls, points to a significant endowment of at least one benevolent family in medieval times. I believe that Ufford was part of an agricultural area that remained relatively unchanged for much of the Medieval and later years, being divided into a series of feudal estates or manors which eventually disintegrated. Even when I grew up, East Anglia – embracing Suffolk, Norfolk and Essex - was still a relatively poor region of Britain. Yet the sense of optimism that pervaded much of my youth, overrode many of the disadvantages which we lived with as a family and as a community.

The historical struggle for financial survival by East Suffolk's farming community gave rise to a number of parish banks being established in the early nineteenth century **"to open to the lower orders** a Place on Deposit for their Small Savings with the Allowance of a Monthly Interest at the rate of 5 per cent and with full Liberty of withdrawing their Money at any Time." This made sense, given that it was difficult for labourers to afford an apothecary's fees. At first these generally catered for sickness and funeral payments, and did not provide for medical attendance. According to the rules of the Ufford New Friendly Society:

"Every person who enters himself into this Society shall be in perfect health and not exceed the age of 35 years; and every person shall pay three shillings and sixpence entrance money, sixpence of which is to be spent and three shillings to go into the box… …if he happens to be sick, lame or blind and thereby rendered incapable of working at his trade or calling, he shall… receive seven shillings and sixpence a week during that illness if it continues not above six months… after the death of any member of this society there shall be paid forty shillings by the stewards out of the chest towards the funeral charges to the widow, friend or relation".

The age and character of our cottage in Ufford – and indeed others in the village - is testimony that Britain has an enormously rich built heritage, yet its safety and future remain precarious, despite the introduction of significant legislation in the last fifty or so years. The neglect/indifference of owners of our rented half of the cottage and the half next door encapsulate the predicament in relation to the surviving integrity of these buildings.

But why should our family as mere tenants have been bothered? Simple! If **we** didn't give a damn, then no one else would have. At the time I was a student with no money, no bank account, parents struggling to make ends meet, and with a whole load more things to be concerned about than the care and protection of the cottage of which we were tenants, and the cottage next door.

I might not have been particularly articulate at the time, and certainly knew little then about building construction or conservation, but I held even then that conservation was about more than conserving Grade 1* buildings such as cathedrals and palaces and mansions. This category of buildings is important as reflecting aspects of our nation's history and cultural and artistic development funded by a wealth of resources, but not the whole story, and the country's heritage would be far poorer were it not for the thousands of vernacular buildings built and occupied by the more ordinary folk of the near- and more-distant past and which constitute our list of Grade 2 buildings. It is rather like saying that we should just have a handful of National Parks and that there is no room for Areas of Outstanding Natural Beauty, National Nature Reserves and Green Belt land, especially since at least one such ANOB eventually became a National Park [New Forest]. We are happy as a nation to capitalize on the earnings generated by overseas visitors, too easily forgetting that it is our countryside and built heritage that underpins our tourism earnings, not to mention our sanity! Given the protracted delays in the listing of our cottage and other buildings and structures in Ufford, I have to smile when I note in the `official history' of the village that the lower part is now a Conservation Area and that there are numerous listed buildings scattered around, dating from the 16th century, including a traditional long house near Ufford Crown.

Buildings are expensive to repair and maintain, and we were glad that Major Blois Brooke, as our initial landlord in Ufford, had the means and the preparedness to repair buildings occupied by his tenants. We couldn't have, and that's for sure! Besides which, as tenants, having buildings-insurance was not something that we could do, even if we could have afforded it. True, we didn't have a water supply indoors or electricity in the bedrooms, nor did we have a water-closet toilet or a bath/shower. But our rent was affordable and still gave mum enough latitude to maintain a variety in our diet and have fresh meat or sausages on most days. We had a pantry behind the kitchen, which was always cool, if not cold, so things like bread and butter and milk were OK there throughout the year. We kept bread in a large rectangular metal bread tin, with its metal lid, which stood on the stone floor of the pantry; but the trouble with that was that it became too prone to attack from mice that managed to lift off the top and have a good nibble at the small brown Hovis loaves and large white loaves inside! Dad subsequently made a small food storage box with a perforated metal `window' on one side, and which sat on a shelf at shoulder-height; this seems to have solved that problem! However, birds would delight in pecking the metal foil tops of the milk bottles left by the milkman on our front door step, but the use of upturned old cups or plastic mugs subsequently prevented the theft [by the birds, of course!] of the delicious cream that sat on top of the [then] un- homogenized milk!

When an autumn storm in the late 1950s brought down a huge limb of the mature ash tree in our front garden during the night, it fell through the clay pan-tiled roof of the cottage [luckily] between our bedroom and mum's. The fact that the tree was still in full-leaf contributed to the branch being torn off by the high winds. Not only did the tree-limb have to be cut down to size and lowered to the ground outside, but the roof had to be made water-proof, both on a temporary- and permanent-basis. So, whilst as village kids, and somewhat to the Major's annoyance, we loved in earlier years to play hide-and-seek around his sunken garden and pavilion, we were, as tenants, truly appreciative of the prompt remedial action which he and his agent Mr Mitchell took this time round!

It seems that, in line with many villages in sufficiently close proximity to cities like London, Ufford was subsequently to go through the process of 'gentrification', resulting in many of its valuable vernacular buildings being adapted as well as being listed; and even if there were necessary modifications in order that the cottages could be provided with all the 'modern conveniences', the buildings were at least being returned to a state of good repair and the alterations would (hopefully) have been agreed beforehand with the conservation planners. The all-embracing category of '**group-value'** often became the means by which these cottages acquired Grade 2 listed status, even though - or perhaps because (!) - we would be witnessing a spiralling in their market-value as the socio-economic metamorphosis of the village proceeded apace.

Up till the 1960's there was only one statutory-recognised category of Listed Building, which broadly covered the 'crème de la crème' of buildings built for the wealthy landowners, be they the Church or the Aristocracy. The Government had created a non-statutory class of buildings which covered structures that, although not considered sufficiently important to be given statutory protection, were considered worth recognition. This was the situation which we found ourselves in when we sought to protect the cottage we lived in and that of our immediate neighbour from the wanton vandalism of the new owner of the cottages. The other half of our cottage had become empty following the death of Ted Taylor and the re-homing of his wife in an institution, and the owner chose to dismantle the elaborate Tudor brick chimney stack serving that empty property, seemingly without good reason. He was able to do that because neither that cottage nor ours had <u>statutory protection,</u> which, anyhow, they were unlikely to have been granted at the time. After all, adopting the thinking behind early listed building categorisation, if not subsequent thinking, they were still seen as mere examples of simple vernacular building, and, as such, of little consequence in built-heritage terms. I still recall how, in the early 1990s, during a prolonged building industry recession – and at the point in time when I was completing my MSc in Construction Management - I sought to get to the bottom of why the House of Commons Select Committee responsible for the built heritage was not putting its weight behind any efforts to prevent so many of the country's skilled building tradesmen from being forced to leave the industry. We call that process `**deskilling.**'

I was anticipating becoming an Architect/Landscape Architect/Project Management Consultant on the completion of the course, and during part of my research, I recall receiving a disappointingly non-committal response from the Chairman of the said Committee, notwithstanding that the proper repair of the nation's traditional building stock depended on these skilled tradesmen, and the fact that we as a nation would not be able to replace this valuable skills-bank for years. Governments are elected for a maximum of five years at a time, and `short-term' policies therefore too often take precedence, whatever the longer-term consequences.

But a word of caution seems not to go amiss here: many, if not all, Local Authorities own a good number of both Grade 1 and Grade 2 Listed buildings and a worrying proportion of these are doubly at risk because of a possible conflict of interests, whereby the defaulting Local Authority[s] is both `judge and jury.' Furthermore, protective planning mechanisms which might hitherto have been regarded as sufficiently robust in relation to listed buildings are now more susceptible, as we witness the further dilution of the planning system and its resourcing. I am alluding here to the recent *Enterprise and Regulatory Reform Act*. English Heritage is obliged to advise the public that *Certificates of Immunity* [COIs] can be applied for by building owners fearful that their properties might be listed before redevelopment proposals run their normal course:

[They] *"are a useful tool where development is intended on a site ....listing a building at a late stage in the preparations of planning proposals can cause delay and other hardships to owners, and even the abandonment of redevelopment schemes......by applying for a certificate they can establish either that they have five years to carry out their development without the possibility of listing interrupting their programme, or that if the buildings gets listed as part of the COI process, they must seek listed building consent for the alteration, extension or demolition of the building."*

According to my brother's recollection, the first property on the land sold by Blois Brooke's executors was built near the gates in Ufford Place, in the early 1960s, and the much larger scale redevelopment as a private housing estate followed. This reflected a change in the social fabric of the village which was largely a consequence of the changing economic and employment situation. In my childhood there was a good handful of small-scale farming families scattered around the village. I well remember the plough-shares being drawn by Suffolk Shire horses, and these were gradually replaced by smallish tractors as farming families tried to make ends meet. I well remember the Orfords farming in their small way near the beginning of East Lane and their motive power for ploughing and pulling the hay-wagons was still the horse. They couldn't afford tractors.

My best mate Michael Miller's father Mark was a cattle truck driver for Carters, the local hauliers, and Mr Taylor, whose family lived next door to them, was the dairyman on the adjoining farm. But farming was changing and fields were getting larger with the growing use of mechanical machinery. It became increasingly more difficult to employ farm-labourers outside of the farmer's family in those days, and I shall never forget how, as I understood it, one farmer, in desperation, took their own life.

In the summer and autumn, many villagers earned precious money picking blackcurrants on Sheepshanks' Decoy Farm on Lower Road or plums on the large orchard the other side of the A12 main road [Upper Street] in Ufford. And the elderly Dredge sisters - who lived in a bungalow up School Lane from the Barrack Corner just before it meets the Avenue - collected blackberries picked by villagers for pin-money, as with acorns destined for pig-feeding. We were always happy to knock on their door and proudly hand over our hard-earned fruit- and acorn harvests, ready to be weighed on their old-fashioned scales, and then to be paid real pocket money for our efforts. We villagers also used to pick plums for money on a fruit farm in the vicinity of Hungarian Hall and Byng Hall Road, which lies on the west side of what used to be the A12 Trunk Road, and could be reached as the continuation of School Lane across the main road. The logical destination for the plums would have been the [*Turban* brand] Canning Factory at Woodbridge, and the blackberries might well have been sent to Chivers of Cambridge, for making into jam. Jam is still produced by the successors to the company, using the *Hartley's* brand-name.

The *East Anglian Daily Times* of April 28th 2007 was to print this item immediately following Captain Sheepshanks' death: "Warm tributes were paid last night to one of Suffolk's best known characters, who made a massive contribution to the county over more than 50 years. Captain Robin Sheepshanks CBE died peacefully at home in Eyke [over the railway crossing from Ufford and a bit further along the road!] near Woodbridge on Wednesday following an 18-month battle with a blood cancer called myeloma." Unbeknown to me at the time, Captain Sheepshanks was Head of the Board of Governors at Farlingaye School, Woodbridge, which my brother and I attended.

There was a time when there were only four or so cars in the village, owned respectively by the village post-master, a Justice of the Peace, a `comfortably-off' lady and our Sunday School teacher. Everybody else got around on pedal bikes or on foot, with trips to Woodbridge, Ipswich and beyond being on the bus. Whilst the Ipswich – Lowestoft railway line passed through the outlying part of Ufford, astride the Eyke road, there was no station, only a railway level-crossing which I remember being manned by Mrs. Agnes Pitcher [née Lincoln] and her husband Basil. She and her older son Barry/Barrie will also be well remembered for organising Socials at the church hall down our lane, and this was a very popular event which served to unite the village community across the whole age range. The music was provided by a visiting DJ, who travelled around on his very powerful BMW 1000 motorbike, and his vinyl records were amplified by huge speakers. Barry Pitcher was born in Loddon in neighbouring Norfolk in the summer of 1938, and who married in 1962, worked for a while from W.H.Smith's newspaper stall at Woodbridge railway station, and would deliver newspapers in Ufford. Christopher, who is Barry's younger brother, was born in 1948 near Wickham Market, a short drive north up the A12 from Ufford. He married Dianna in 1966. Mrs. Pitcher also had two daughters, Daphne, who was born in 1929 in Loddon, near Norwich, and died in 1988, and Barbara, also born in Loddon about a year later and married in 1954. I think that at least one of the daughters had left home by the time that John and I were kids playing with friends in the village. But Mrs. Pitcher was as keen at spotting misbehaviour as spotting approaching trains, because, after more than 55 years, my brother has

owned up to being reported   by Mrs. Pitcher to the local
police for throwing pieces of wood into the river near Ufford
bridge. And who was the other accomplice? Evidently it was
Keith Y, who I think belonged to the same Melton Boy Scouts
Group as us at the time. And did mum know? Apparently not!

Then we had Ufford Football Club, which played its home-
games on the flood-prone meadow adjacent to the bridge
crossing the River Deben. All the players had to change in the
bar of the Lion pub, some 300 or so yards up the road, and
whilst there were no such things as showers, the players
indulged in a pint of beer. Cyril Chilvers was publican at the
time, and he also ran a roof-thatching business which is still in
operation and is now based in neighbouring Pettistree. Cyril
was born in 1911 and married Daphne Ward in 1948. He died
in 1981. The football team's manager was Fred Nicholls – and
I will always remember the towering figure of his son `Huxter'
- and among the players I recall as being outstanding were
brothers Justin and Jeremy Smith from neighbouring
Wickham Market. Dick came from Grundisburgh and Reggie
Massingham from upper Ufford. Reggie, who was born in
Dunmow in Essex in 1920, was one of the senior members of
the team. By the time that I was around seventeen, I was
playing for my Civic College team, and I had my doubts about
how well that went down with my peer-friends in Ufford, in
terms of club loyalty! Reggie and his wife [née Last] had five
children: Trevor [b.1953], Lynn [b.1947], Jill [b.1959], Theresa
[b.1961] and Trudi [b.1965]. Sadly, Trevor died in a road
accident near the Crown Inn in Upper Ufford – on what was
the A12 main road -in early 1958.

Other villagers I recollect were the Slacks and the Booths.
Agnes Slack died in Ipswich in 1962 at the age of 93 and James
W.E Slack died locally in late 1960 at the age of 69. I would
not be surprised if Percy Frederick Booth was a close relative
of Mrs. Booth. Born in Ufford, he sacrificed his life on the
battlefield in the First World War and is commemorated both
on the Ploegsteert Memorial in Belgium and on a plaque in

Ufford Church. The Ploegsteert Memorial commemorates more than 11,000 servicemen of the United Kingdom and South African forces who died in this sector during the First World War and have no known grave. Most of those commemorated by the memorial did not die in major offensives, such as those which took place around Ypres to the north or Loos to the south, but in the course of the day-to-day trench warfare which characterized this part of the line, or in small scale set engagements, usually carried out in support of the major attacks taking place elsewhere.

There were some really kind, reliable, genuinely decent people in the village that mum made good friends with, including the Oxborrows, whose children Martyn and Kay were our age, and Mrs. Booth, who lived next to the Crown Public House on what used to be the A12 main road in Upper Ufford. A Sergeant Horace Oxborrow was also from Ufford, and his military service in World War 1 is recorded in the Imperial War Museum's records. Kay married locally into the Adair family in the March quarter of 1967. I believe that the Oxborrows moved to Ransom Road, near Farlingaye School at the time that the children reached secondary school age.

During the Second World War, the Government had constructed a Nissan Hut camp at the upper end of the Blois-Brook's local estate, and, because of the dire shortage of social housing at the cessation of the war, the local district council had acquired these Nissan huts and let them out to families. I had a small number of friends who lived with their parents in these homes and can still recall how cosy they were.

Once in a while, I would take the bus to the cinema in Woodbridge with Bernard Walton and his dad, and after watching the films. Bernard's dad would delight in catching us both unawares by dinging our ears when we weren't looking. Bernard and I would be treated to a fish-and-chip supper by Bernard's dad, with the take-away meal wrapped up in newspaper to keep it warm. The chip shop was a stone's throw from the cinema and the adjacent railway station, at the bottom of Quay Street. In those days, the potatoes were peeled and cut-up by a huge machine at the back of the premises, whereas today the pre-cut chipped potatoes arrive in large, sealed polythene bags, ready to be emptied into the scorching hot vegetable oil in the fryer. We would get off the bus at Ufford Park and walk down the concrete road to the Waltons' Nissen hut home, whence I would wend my way home via School Lane and Barrack Corner. Sometimes Bernard and I were taken to the speedway at Foxhall Stadium near Ipswich, where we would watch in awe as the likes of World Champion Ove Funden, generally representing his Norwich team, whizzed around the track on their motorbikes at break-neck speed, defying the laws of gravity as they lent into the bends. I remember that on one occasion, the Ipswich Witches were challenging Wolverhampton, and on that night the three Beverley Sisters, who were a renowned singing trio at the time, came along to support Wolverhampton. After all, England soccer captain Billy Wright played for Wolverhampton Wanderers, and his girlfriend was one of the Beverley Sisters! The Foxhall Stadium was purpose-built for speedway in 1950 and at peak times nearly 20,000 people packed in to experience the excitement and exhilaration of the speedway. My cousins Sylvia, Sonia and Stella, along with their parents, made the short move from Kesgrave to Rushmere village, which is close to the stadium.

We kids spent many a school holiday playing in the woods of Ufford Place, and from time to time ventured to come out from the cover of the trees and play on the Major's croquet lawn or slide down the low, sloping brick wall running down the side of the steps leading into the sunken garden. If we were spotted by the Major, we would receive a stern reprimand and promise in return not to enter the grounds of the manor again. That said, this remained for us as children as the quickest way to reach the homes of the families living in the Nissan huts, as long as we could scale the high brick wall adjoining the gates at the entrance to Ufford Place. The wall was built in Flemish bond but omitting the headers, and so we had a foothold, even though the Major was subsequently to keep the gates locked. The drastically cut-back version of that wall that now replaces it – probably altered for the sake of vehicle sight-lines - loses a lot of the beauty and character of the old brick wall.

The present housing estate, called Parklands, was part of the original park that belonged to Ufford Place, Colonel Blois Brook's Ufford estate. During WWII it was requisitioned by the army for the use of tanks and guns.

After World War II ended in 1945 the newly elected Labour government under Mr Clement Attlee faced big reconstruction problems. Not the least was an acute housing shortage brought about by bomb damage and general lack of maintenance. By the early 1950s young married demobilized servicemen and their wives were starting families and expected something better than having to live with parents or in-laws. Financially the country was broke after the crippling cost of six years of war, and house building materials were in very short supply. What was to be done? One temporary solution lay in the colonies of Nissen Huts being vacated by service personnel from units that were disbanding. The huts were painted black and were fitted out with amenities for a family - stove, bath, two bedrooms, kitchen, the toilet and an outside coal bunker. The families that I remember living there were Ian Stammers and his parents, Brian Flatman and his parents, Bernard Walton and his parents, Keith Dawson, his brother and parents and Kate Bloomfield and her parents. The Nissen hut camp in Ufford Park was eventually replaced by conventionally-built new social housing, and the land on which the manor house stood was developed as housing for sale. Concrete bases of Nissan huts used as barracks can still be seen in the woods on this area.

Before researching this book, I did not know that my village of Ufford had welcomed evacuees from Grays in

Eastern London/Essex at the outbreak of the war in 1939, yet moving from London, as THE prime bombing target, to the East Coast of England did not come without its risks. Someone a few years old than me and who grew up in a village near Ufford, recalled that in later years she and her family/friends realised that much of the security-risk in this area during the war was related to the RAF station at Bawdsey Manor, about four miles down the road from them. In the BBC series 'The Peoples' War', Mary Davies stated on 18th September, 2003: "The area was classified as safe in 1939, and crowds of evacuees from London's East End descended on the village. The village school had to be shared between us; the evacuees attending in the mornings and the village children in the afternoons. This was the time of the *Phoney War* when nothing seemed to happen, and many of the children drifted back to London in the first few months. In May 1940 everything changed when Hitler invaded Holland and Belgium. People living on the East Anglian coast realised just how near to home the war had come and everyone was saying fearfully 'It'll be our turn next.' The evacuees in the area were moved away speedily to safer places and civilians were advised to leave whenever possible. Even before the war [Bawdsey Manor] had been a top-security establishment. It later transpired that Bawdsey Manor was the power-house behind the development of Radar, which had such important implications, not only in the defeat of the Luftwaffe, but in worldwide communications since. This was all very hush-hush at the time, of course, and all sorts of rumours were rife about magic rays that could bring down enemy planes. They weren't far wrong!" During a 50 year reunion in 1989, an Evacuees' oak tree was planted in Ufford in commemoration of the reception of evacuees from Grays. Bawdsey RAF was also to be critical as an East Coast look-out station watching out 24/7 for an air-attack from the Soviet Union even early on in the Cold War, and one of our near neighbours in Church

Lane was an RAF officer engaged in that task at Bawdsey at the time.

The whole of this part of the East Coast was similarly critical and susceptible in relation to the World War Two campaign. Later on I will be mentioning RAF/USAAF Martlesham Heath, USAF Bentwaters and RAF Woodbridge. All these are particularly close to the Deben Estuary and the coast, but there was also Debach, a bit further inland. Debach lies in the heart of Suffolk, near Charlsfield, Dalinghoo and Wickham Market, and about 3 miles north-west of Woodbridge. Indeed it is still relatively isolated today in the undulating and relatively unspoilt Suffolk countryside, despite the `metamorphosis' of many parts of [East] Suffolk, including Ufford. With some of the airfield located in the adjoining village of Burgh, Debach was one of the last 8th Air Force heavy bomber stations to be occupied by the American 8th Army Air Force. Apparently, the pronunciation of Debach was always a problem for uninitiated Americans, who invariably referred to "Dee-bark", whereas locals [and former-locals like me] have always pronounced it as "Deb-idge". The airfield, which was subsequently to house German prisoners-of-war in 1945,closed soon after the war but part of the runway has been preserved and it has, in part, been restored in commemoration of its war-time significance and in memory of the brave men who served there. The flight-observation tower also survives on the horizon.

My wife Lynne, my brother John and I approached Debach cross-country from Needham Market, and with the aid of a sat-nav. If I was to try to trace the hamlet of Debach today, starting instead from Ufford, and without the assistance of a satnav or a map, I guess that I might head down the road leading from the [former A12 main]-road at the *Pettistree Three Tuns* public-house cross-roads. This was roughly the route [in reverse] that John and I took when we were cycling home cross-country from Newmarket, having alighted from the train from Edinburgh [via Peterborough and

Cambridge] after cycling and youth-hostelling round the Scottish highlands in the summer holiday of 1959.

The pair of semi-detached cottages where we lived in Church Lane, Ufford, and now known as Lady Cottages, was occupied by our family and by Ted Taylor, the village roadman, and his wife Violet. The small kitchen in our half of the cottage had a stone floor, a very low ceiling, a black coal-fired oven range and a copper boiler with its own fire-compartment underneath. There was also a living room on the ground floor, a pantry and a coal-cupboard under the stair. There were two small bedrooms upstairs, reached by a tiny winding stair and a narrow landing at the top. Each of the bedrooms was lit by a small dormer window. The pair of cottages themselves probably dates back to the sixteenth or seventeenth century, and was constructed as a timber frame with wattle-and-daub infill walls, a red pan-tiled clay roof and a pair of elaborate Tudor-style chimney stacks. The bay-window to the living room in our half of the cottages overlooked the croquet lawn of a Mrs. Morris, who had a large brick-built detached house and gardens next to us.

Our semi-detached cottage had been rented to us since 1945, shortly after I had been born. The cottage had been a tied estate-cottage for workers on the Blois Brooke manor, and comprised a kitchen, a living room and two small bedrooms reached by a narrow winding stairway. We moved in around late summer, having spent a short while as guests of my late Uncle Alf and his family at Kesgrave, near Ipswich. Their family, comprising Uncle Alf, Aunty Nancy and daughters Sylvia, Stella and Sonia, lived in a modest bungalow not so far back from the A12 trunk road that wended its way north from Ipswich and passed through the upper part of Ufford on its way to Lowestoft and Great Yarmouth. I am not sure when Alf had moved south to Kesgrave in Suffolk, but by the close of the Second World War in the second week of May, 1945, Alf had already created a home for his wife and daughters. Uncle Alf was quite a bit older than my father, who had been the seventh surviving child of Alexander and Alice Hutchinson, who had lived in Tynemouth, Northumberland.

Before we moved into the cottage, we had stayed a short while as guests of my late uncle Alf and his family at their bungalow in Kesgrave, near Ipswich, which was about nine miles away from our cottage. Our cottage had been empty at the time that peace was declared in Europe, and precisely because it was empty, the Lord of the Manor was obliged to make it available to families re-entering `Civvies'-life' and who, furthermore, now found themselves homeless. I recollect that my late mother had called in at the Deben Rural District Council offices on Melton Hill in Woodbridge, three or so miles from Ufford, and had been informed of the availability of the cottage to rent. There was no electricity laid on at the time that we moved in, nor any mains cold water or main-drain w.c. In fact, it was some twelve or so years before the cottage on the roadside of our garden path was provided with a septic tank, but we had to make do with lowering a bucket down a brick well in our near-neighbour's garden (via our immediate neighbour's garden path) until we were provided with a cold-water standpipe in our front garden, and had use our immediate neighbour's garden path again to reach our privy-midden bucket-toilet attached to one side of our garden shed, which again was off this neighbour's access path. So, late on Sunday night, preferably after dark, my late father would empty the contents of the toilet bucket into a hole that he or John or I had dug that day on our part of the allotment gardens outside our garden gate. The barn-shed pertaining to our immediate neighbour, Ted Taylor, adjoined our own garden shed. Today there is mains sewage disposal in Church Lane, and the drinking-water well structure has gone from Mrs. Jenvey's garden, save for the stone that covers the disused well.

Without wanting to exaggerate, I suggest that, in many respects, people were better off living in the town of Woodbridge both during and immediately after the end of the

War. In his recollections of life as a child in Woodbridge during the war, for the BBC ` Our Families' War series, John E Moreton wrote:

"One evening when we were under the table, during an air raid, my Granddad, went out with a white tin basin on his head, which doubled as his tin hat watching the bombers go over to bomb London, and it was just getting dark, Now picture the scene, our toilet being at the bottom of our garden and no more than a bucket sunk into the ground, with a wooden seat above, housed in a 3 ft sq. red brick building with no door and a tin roof. These buckets were large and were emptied by the "Night Soils men" who came along in special lorries about once a week. As the poor man walked up our garden path, with the bucket on his shoulder, granddad shouted in something in Gaelic, which gave him such a fright that the man jumped out of his skin, the bucket slipped, and the man ended up being covered in a week's worth of family compost!. When we found out we split our sides with laughter. However the next day he "the man" came and tried to give granddad a good punching, but he reckoned without my Mum's Irish Temper. "

And then there are the unprompted but vivid recollections shared with us by Heather, my dear second cousin on my dad's side of the family, whom my wife Lynne and I, along with John, went to meet at our cousin Stan's home in September 2014. Heather well remembers travelling down with her parents and other family members from North Shields in Northumberland to Ufford to visit my dad in the 1970s, before he gave up the cottage. There was only room for a small number of people to sleep over in the cottage, and Heather was one of those. The others were kindly put up in the more modern home of Dougie Goldsmith, who, at the time, was dad's employer in the tree and shrub nurseries at the other end of the village. And, since nothing had changed since John, Mum and I had left home, dad's visitors had the questionable pleasure of walking to the outdoor latrine through our neighbour's garden. To Heather's relief, dad realised that things needed to be more refined, and he provided her with a receptacle on the upstairs landing of the cottage. I don't know whether mains drainage had reached Church Lane Ufford by the time of Heather's childhood visit, but clearly our cottage had not by then be connected up by then. Yet I do remember that the painted cottage next to Mrs. Jenvey's, which used to be occupied by Terry Woods and his family, was linked to a small new septic tank in the early 1960s, and this tank was placed by the cottage-owners on the allotment to the left of the path leading up to our home and that of Ted Taylor. Periodically, the small road tanker would stop outside our roadside gate, and sucking would commence! Terry Woods was privileged to have had that facility, but now all the residents of Church Lane can enjoy mains gas as well as mains drainage! I guess that we now take this too much for granted, taking the world-view.

The truth of the matter was that towns such as Woodbridge had enjoyed mains drainage for very many years, and all my school pals' homes on the housing estates at the edge of the town had this facility as a matter of course. And after a football/sports lesson at Farlingaye School, we could enjoy a hot shower. It needed considerable investment to bring mains drainage to lower Ufford, and tenants like ourselves were helpless in this matter, for if the Deben Rural District Council [as the predecessor Suffolk Coastal District], even as the agent of Central Government, was not prepared to make that investment in the 1950s, 60s and 70s, and the private landlords of cottages such as our own were not prepared, in the interim, to provide septic tanks, then tough!

3 PIECING TOGETHER MY FAMILY JIGSAW PUZZLE AND MY VILLAGE COMMUNITY

Chances are that I will never know exactly where, when and how my parents met. Cousin Stan thinks that dad and mum met at a club in London when dad was in London on leave during the war. Dad was, after all, an infantryman with the Middlesex Regiment! And if there is a stereotypical family unit, then I don't think that ours was! And whilst most of my relatives on my dad's side live up on Tyneside, relatives on my late mum's side were, for all intents and purposes, non-existent.

Whilst I have to confess that for very many years I was not in contact with my dad's relations, my northern cousins would also concede that they too are not in regular contact with each other either. However I am grateful that my paternal cousins have, in recent years, magnanimously shared some recollections of my dad and have kindly given me a family tree on his side of the family, In fact, when my wife Lynne and I first met-up with them some years ago, one of them admitted that she did not know my dad by his proper name [Harold Octavious] and had to be reminded by her Geordie cousins that he **was** the 'Charlie' that had been mentioned on occasion amongst her and her cousins.

Our dad was born Harold Octavius Hutchinson on June 21st 1913, the last of a large family, all but one of whom had been boys. His father had worked in the shipbuilding industry on Tyneside, but by the time that my father was just over 14 years of age, he had become an orphan and was placed in the Tynemouth Workhouse, alongside his next youngest brother

Sep [Septimus].   Luckily, his sister Alice, one of the older children - though she was a young lady by then - rescued him from the Workhouse and looked after him and Sep as young teenagers, remaining a close and trusted sister for the rest of her life. In fact, Alice seems to have taken charge of the remaining household when the last of her parents died, and she was allowed to bring both my dad and his brother Sep back home from the workhouse at the weekends, as long as one of the members of the family was bringing in enough money to feed them all.

The first children born to my father's parents were twin boys, viz: George Baden Powell Hutchinson and Martin Kitchener Hutchinson. Sadly, they died within their first year of life. The subsequent children were Albert, Alfred, Ormond (Stanley), Sydney, Alice, Septimus …… and finally my dad Harold Octavius, known affectionately as `Charlie' by the rest of his side of the family. My father met my mother in London during the Second World War, presumably when he was on leave and my mother was working in the Capital. My older brother John was conceived around Christmas, 1942, and, to put that into context, it would be another eighteen or so months before my dad was to take part in the D-Day landings on the Normandy beaches.

In 2003, I had written a speculative letter to the Editor of the *Evening Star* newspaper in Ipswich a little while before, asking if any of his readership knew of my cousins who had lived as children in nearby Kesgrave, and this letter led to an article in the paper shortly afterwards. I include that article below:

Friday, May 23, 2003
6:42 AM
Bonza! Star reunites farflung family

FOUR cousins who live on opposite sides of the world have been reunited - thanks to The Evening Star.

Michael Hutchinson wrote a letter to *The Star* in April asking for help in tracing part of his family, formerly of Cambridge Road, Kesgrave, who he had not seen for more than 50 years.

When he began his search, he never thought sisters Stella Guy, Sonia Hodgson and Sylvia Kirk (all nee Hutchinson) would be living nearly 10,000 miles away in Australia.

But distance proved to be no barrier as a former colleague of Stella, 62, who worked at Footman's department store, in Ipswich, read Mr. Hutchinson's plea and passed on Stella's contact details.

Marina Potter, 68, of Selkirk Road, Ipswich, who visited Stella in Australia nine years ago, said: "I read the letter and just rang the number. The man was so pleased to hear from me."

The 57-year-old was then able to make a surprise phone call to his long-lost cousin, who lives within 12 miles of her two sisters Sonia, 61, and Sylvia, 65, in Mandurah, West Australia.

He said: "It was quite a shock to find out she was living in Australia and a shock that we traced them so easily. "We had given up hope of the reunion ever happening and it wouldn't have worked without *The Star*."

Mr Hutchinson, who lived with his cousins in Kesgrave for a short time after World War Two, then moved to Ufford before leaving the area to study in London.

He now lives in Huddersfield and is busy making plans with his wife, Lynne, for a reunion trip to Australia to meet all three cousins.

"We're quite excited about going over to Australia and meeting up after such a long time," said Mr Hutchinson, who is in regular contact with Stella via e-mail.

Sylvia emigrated to Australia in the 1960s, while her sister Sonia followed suit in 1983, two years after Stella uprooted.

Stella said: "I was very surprised to hear from Michael. It was such a coincidence that he called as I have recently started tracing my family tree.

"We're so pleased and excited to be in touch that some of us may well visit the UK in the not too distant future to meet some of the family."

When Marina rang me, she said that she had been a school-friend of Stella and that all of the sisters had long since migrated to Western Australia. My subsequent exchange of emails with Stella allowed us to exchange life-stories as well as for her to reveal events surrounding my cousins' parents that came as quite a shock to me. Cousin Stan from Tynemouth tells me that the sisters did make the long trip back to the UK a few years ago to visit cousins living on Tyneside.

My father was a quiet, withdrawn person, who was happy to sit in his deck-chair in our childhood cottage garden, potter about in the garden and on the allotment, and enjoy his pint of Cobbold's locally-brewed beer - with friends like Maureen Murphy's dad Edward - on Saturday nights at the Crown Inn on Upper Street at the other end of the village. Maureen was born in Newmarket, in mid-Suffolk, in 1940, the daughter of Edward Murphy and wife Doreen (née Smith). Maureen married Philip Pendle (b. 1945) in Ipswich in 1971

Generally speaking, my dad did not drink to excess, although my brother and I still chuckle over the occasion on one Christmas eve when we both went to the midnight service at the church down our lane, only to be greeted there by our dad, stumbling in somewhat 'worse for wear'!

From as far back as I remember, both my parents had needed to go out to work to bring in money for the family to get by. My dad had been a builder's labourer with Frank Ingram Smith, a Woodbridge building firm, and mum worked for some years at the Woodbridge Canning Factory near the cinema and close to the riverside and railway station. During the winter, the factory used to pack dates imported from North Africa and elsewhere.

Dad had usually left for work on his pedal cycle by the time that the rest of us had risen on weekday mornings, having made his `regulation' white bread, margarine and cheese sandwiches before he went to bed the previous evening, leaving only the making his flask of tea before he set off.

My parents had different sets of friends. Whilst my dad's friends were `drinking mates', mum's were generally youngish mothers like herself, who lived nearby in the lower village. There was the Easty family who lived in School Lane, and the Birt family who lived a few doors down from them. The Easty's had two daughters: Heather the older sister, and Helen, and they were about the same age as my brother and me. Heather, the older sister, attended Ufford County Primary School, then went on to the larger school at Wickham Market when she turned eleven years. Her sister Helen likewise went to Ufford School before passing her 11+ exams and moving on to the publically-funded Felixstowe Grammar School.

The Grimble family lived next to the Race family, a few yards up the road from the village post office and general store, and their younger children played with us at the weekends and during the school holidays. Mr and Mrs. Grimble married in the September quarter of 1941, and Mr Grimble worked on the local dust-carts. Rita Jackson, the oldest of Mrs. Grimble's children, was born in Ipswich [probably at the hospital] in the September quarter of 1936. Anne Grimble, the second oldest of Mrs. Grimble [née Barker]'s children after Rita Jackson, was born in Ipswich in the December quarter of 1941, and, like her sister Susan, married in 1971. Susan married in Westminster (London) into the Mackie family. Freda Grimble was born in 1946. Freddy was born in 1948 and Linda Grimble was born in 1953. Sheila, who is about my age, was to marry one of the USAF servicemen from the nearby American airbase, and to settle in the States.

Dinah [Patricia D. Wright, née Grimble] married locally in 1960. Freddie [Frederick G Grimble] was to marry locally to Roberta Adams family in 1970, and Susan Grimble married locally into the Tiller family in 1972. 'Granny' [Mrs. Emma] Barker died in the March quarter of 1956, age 81, as did Thomas A. Barker, aged 84.

There are two distinct parts to the village of Ufford: firstly, the western part, where development is centred on Upper Street, which formed part of the London to Great Yarmouth A12 trunk road until the [second] by-pass was built; and secondly, the original core of the village where we lived, in around St Mary's Church. These two parts of the village are linked by School Lane, and by Spring Lane. In our youth, the two components of the village were separated by Blois Brooke's Ufford Place estate, at the top end of which was Ufford Park, which, with its wartime Nissan huts, became a council estate after the war. There were two groups of purpose-built council houses in the village, both in the upper or western part. One was just up the road from the Crown Inn, and opposite the farmer's field which Dougie Goldsmith was to develop as a plant nursery. The other larger component was further north along the old A12, in the direction of Pettistree and Wickham Market.

The families in and around Ufford who we counted as friends, included the Pawseys, the Last's [Graham was born in late 1941], the Hines's [Greta was our age] and the Downings. My brother and I remember Bernard Downing, who was born in Woodbridge in the June quarter of 1933, and Bob Downing, who married a Freeman in the area in the June quarter of 1957. Then there were the Micklewrights, including son Colin, and the Oxborrow family, including twins Martyn and Kay, who were born in the September quarter of 1945. Mrs. Oxborrow [née Hansley] and dad Kenneth Oxborrow were married in the June quarter of 1938 and they moved from Ufford to Ransome Road, Woodbridge, near Farlingaye School, before the twins were due to start at that school. Kay married the slightly older Michael Adair locally in the Spring of 1967 and Martyn married Catherine Last in Ipswich in the Spring of 1968.

The Foremans and the Bradleys lived on Spring Lane or close to it. Rodney Foreman played in the unofficial lower village's junior football team that I rounded up, and was a particularly talented member, alongside Michael Miller. Rodney [J] Foreman was born in the December quarter of 1946 and was about the same age as Michael Miller. He married Wendy Abbott in 1969. His sister Joyce was born in the spring of 1945, and married into the Finch family in the spring of 1966. [Mrs. Miller was born a Finch]. Yvonne Foreman was born in early 1948 and Angela Foreman died at the young age of 17 in late 1960.

Margaret Bradley [née Wood] came from Sheffield, married Harold Bradley in the late summer of 1937 and had two sons, Jack and Bobby. Jack was born in Sheffield in the December quarter of 1939, around the time of Britain's declaration of war against Germany. Given that Mr Bradley was likely to have been called up for National Service at the outbreak of the war and that his wife had a baby boy born just at that point, it would have been risky for Mrs. Bradley to have stayed in Sheffield. As one of Britain's most important industrial cities during the war, Sheffield would have been one of Hitler's prime targets. Bobby was born in/near Ufford in the September quarter of 1946, a little more than a year after me. It might well be that he was born at the Phyllis Memorial Maternity Home, which was situated where the back road from Ufford to Melton meets the Woodbridge to Upper Ufford and Wickham Market road.

My brother John and I had begun 'proper school-life' at Ufford County Primary, although mum had sent us both for a short while to the Deben Bank nursery school when we were 3-4 years old.

Schools were a major bone of contention between our parents, and were, according to my brother, a contributory cause of the violent flare-ups at home when I was a kid.

Ufford School was a place of happy memories for both John and me. Indeed, my brother John continued at Ufford Primary until he was eleven before transferring to Wickham Market Area School, which was co-educational and took pupils from five-years old to fifteen. The head teacher was Miss Dee, who lived on Melton Hill, Woodbridge. Mum was a good friend of Ms. Shipp, one of the Ufford School teachers, who lived in a cute but distinctive round brick house in the village of Easton. This village lay slightly off the beaten track, the other side of Wickham Market, and from time to time we [that is, my mother, brother and I] would be invited there for tea and cake.

Ufford School closed quite a few years ago and is now a private residence. The original school building has high ceilings reaching up to the pitched roof, and had large, coal-fired heaters in at least one of the classrooms. The influx of children that had resulted from families moving into the Nissan huts, post-war, meant that a pre-fabricated classroom was added on the far side of the playground, and this doubled as a dining hall, with a kitchen at one end separated by a sliding shutter. School Lane ran three hundred or so yards on from the school to me [what was] the A12 main road, but on my recent visit, I noticed that it had been blocked off, and now seemed at a fleeting glance to be part of the garden to the adjoining house.

Virtually all the children attending Ufford School ate school dinners, which were excellently prepared by Mrs. Raven. Parents sent the money with their children to pay for these at the beginning of each week, and the cost of these to the parents was quite affordable even by our standards as a relatively poor family. To say that we children were well catered for really was a truism, even if money was tight at home. One of the highlights of the school-week for us children was when our mum used to stop off at the school gate on her way home from the bus-stop and hand out a box of Smarties to be shared amongst us.

Mrs. Raven, the school-cook, lived with her husband in School Lane, Ufford, and –although I stand to be corrected – I believe they had relatives living towards the bottom of Church Lane, a one minute walk for us, a stone's throw from the village hall. Indeed, their back-garden extended virtually up to the ground where our outdoor earthen closet shed was sited, beyond our neighbour Ted Taylor's garden shed and our own, and an extension of land lying immediately behind our cottage. Violet V Raven died in the locality in the March quarter of 1967, aged 69, and Florence E Raven died in Ipswich in the June quarter of 1965, at the age of 67.

As we grew older, mum entertained the notion that I attended Woodbridge Grammar, but, at the time, this was a 'public' fee-paying school with both boarding- and day-pupils, and was 'boys only', with the Abbey Preparatory School as its feeder school. At secondary school level there was Wickham Market Junior-cum-Secondary School and Felixstowe- and Framlingham Grammars, which at the time were funded by the East Suffolk County Council as the local education authority. Felixstowe was for the boys and Framlingham was for the girls.

Hindsight has perhaps given me a clearer insight into my parents' ways of thinking, because my mum was the 'intellectual' in the family, with a middle-class Jewish background, thus being a great believer in education as the key to success in life. By way of contrast, my dad had working-class roots and values that he cherished. Thus, when I turned seven years old, my mother instigated the process whereby I would be enrolled as a day-boy at the Abbey Preparatory School in Woodbridge, whilst my brother remained at Ufford County Primary. As far as I can recall, all my peers at the Abbey School were from relatively wealthy middle/upper-class backgrounds. School fees were a real issue for my parents, with my mum being in the 'driving seat' but still depending on the co-operation of my dad.

How I survived the four years at the Abbey School I still find amazing, for there wasn't only the question of fees, and the cost of the uniform, sports kit, etc., etc.! All my peers at the school had reasonably well-to-do families, but I had my small group of friends whilst at the school, including Graham Lacey, who lived at the time in Wickham Market with his younger brother and parents. And there was also Richard Stevenson, a farmer's son from Hasketon near Woodbridge. I have joyful recollections of summer holidays spent riding at the back of one of his parents' Fordson tractors, and picking 'monkey bacca' from the hedgerows near the farm. Another good friend was Nigel Broadbent, who lived on Melton Hill, close to where the Headmistress of Ufford Primary School lived.

To say that I was a 'fish out of water' at this boys-only prep school would be an under-statement. I was certainly not headmaster Mr McCarthy's favourite pupil at the Abbey Preparatory School in Woodbridge, although it was not for want of being able to follow lessons in class. We all had to have a freshly washed, bleached and ironed serviette to put in polished metal serviette holder ready for our very formal lunchtime meals in the ancient dining hall of the Tudor school building. It was also a requirement that we pupils 'doffed' our school caps when passing the Headmaster or any of his teaching staff in town, and we would be reprimanded if we did not follow this rule.

As a result of my rebelliousness at school, I was detained on a number of occasions and required to write lines such as The Lord's Prayer a hundred times over. I was also on the receiving end of several bouts of what I considered to be unwarranted caning by Mr. McCarthy in his office. Unsurprisingly, I long regarded this headmaster as sadistic, though, after I had 'flown the Abbey nest' I was quickly able to put the matter behind me. Nevertheless, I accepted from the outset that what I had done was wrong and that I needed to learn my lesson. For the record, in state-run schools, and also in private schools where at least part of the funding came from government, corporal punishment was outlawed by Parliament with effect from 1987. In other private schools in England and Wales, it was banned in 1999.

Whilst I remember sitting the 11+ exam, I don't recollect being shown any exam results at the time. My mother, in many respects the actively responsible parent at that point in time, was sent all correspondence, including exam results, and doubtless would not have wanted to discuss them with dad, given his stance on my ever attending that school in the first place! Anyhow, there was never any question of being expected to 'move up' to the fee-paying Woodbridge (Boys) Grammar School, because, to begin with, my parents couldn't have afforded it.

One of my obsessions at the time was with the *Dinky Toys* owned by some of the pupils who were borders. I began to ` grant a growing number of them a 'safe passage' to my toy-box in my bedroom at home in Ufford. I was thus able to share playing Dinky Toys with my village friends who came around at weekends and during the school holidays, though I was soon to accept that this was a lame excuse for pilfering them in the first place!

Besides which, in the final analysis, I had embarrassed my parents by stealing the Dinky toys. The Headmaster was thus to turn up at our front door in the evening of the last day of my final term, to demand the return of the toys which I had 'sequestered'. I was woken up and called downstairs to duly gather the toys into a bag which mum handed over to Mr McCarthy. Not only did I regret my actions, but, later, genuinely felt sorry for the Headmaster, because he was to lose his wife in childbirth not too long afterwards.

In retrospect, I was intrigued to learn much later that Woodbridge School [of which the Abbey School was a part] had been founded as an independent school in 1577 for the poor of Woodbridge. Strange though it may seem, I did benefit from attending the school. It was a wake-up call, a hard lesson in the art and science of life from which I feel I have benefited. I had also to hold my own when seemingly disadvantaged, as well as taking on board the rules of living. That said, I was happy to let bygones be bygones and begin a new chapter in my life.

Whilst the four years at the Abbey School had largely cut me off from my peers in the village, this was not a complete separation. At weekends and during school holidays, I was still able to play with my friends who lived near us in Lower Ufford, as well as fellow Abbey School friends such as Nigel Broadbent, Richard Stevenson and Graham Lacey - and Woodbridge School – of which the Abbey School is a constituent part - has, notwithstanding my behaviour, evidently granted me the status of 'OW', which means Old Woodbridgian! I was in my last year at the Abbey Preparatory School when John started at Wickham Market Area School, and our mum had 'eyed-up' the educational possibilities for John and me by the time I left that school.

Mum worked in Woodbridge from when I was very young, and did nearly all the family shopping there, generally before she started work in the morning. Generally she would call at Creaseys the butchers - then at the Cross Corner, opposite the Post Office - or Revetts the butchers, Andrews the greengrocers, Wrights the bakers and Gobbitt and Kirby's or Tysons the grocers. I still recall mum producing her rations book at Tysons the grocers in the Thoro'fare in the early 1950s, and the grocer carefully weighing out the cheese and butter and putting the sugar into thick blue paper bags. She did not have to worry, though, about fresh milk and bread, as these were delivered to our doorstep. There was also Toshach's the cycle and radio shop, as well as Hasnip's cycle shop. Mr Alexander Toshach, who was eventually to retire as proprietor of the cycle shop, lived in Bromeswell, up the road from the Ufford railway level-crossing. He died on the 7th

February, 1980, and, fascinatingly, a notice was placed in the London Gazette on the 18th March that year, formally inviting people/businesses contemplating submitting claims, to direct their enquiries to the stated representative of the family's business. This was probably only a legal formality. Hasnips were also to open a cycle shop in Wickham Market, the other side of Ufford, and it is still there. And I should not forget Mr Alexander the outfitter, who, I believe, came to live in Ufford around that time, possibly purchasing Green Tiles next to Ufford Primary School.

Dad liked his white unsliced loaves and we had unsliced Hovis. Our rare treats were baby Hovis loaves. Furthermore, Mr Easty the coalman delivered sacks of coal, and this was stored in the coal-cupboard underneath stairs, and Mr Birt delivered the paraffin we used for the room-heater and for the Primus stove that we cooked on. The galvanised steel cold water bucket, which we filled from the well, stood in one corner of the kitchen, and our kitchen table was covered by a piece of American cloth.

After an electricity supply had been installed in the cottage, Mum bought a *Wee Baby Belling* electric oven, which had a cooking plate on top and which sat on top of the original copper wash-tub, with the electric kettle next to it. And when a cold-water standpipe was provided in our small front-garden, we no longer had to fetch fresh water from the well in Mrs. Jenvy's garden. We washed up in a plastic bowl that also doubled as a washing bowl, with hot water taken from the electric kettle, which had replaced the old fashioned kettle that had stood on the black coal-fired oven that sat in the old fireplace recess. Baths were taken in the small galvanised steel bath that was stored in the coal-cupboard, and the cast-iron clothes iron was heated up on the Primus stove, with the smut carefully wiped off the ironing surface before clothes were ironed.

My mother was not one for sitting down, and she belonged to the local Women's' Institute as well as being

Brown Owl in the village's Brownies group. In 1951, mum took John, I and Peter, the son of one of mum's friends on Ufford Park, on a day trip to London to visit the Festival of Britain, held in the new [Royal] Festival Hall on the South Bank of the Thames, opposite the Houses of Parliament. Like the Great Exhibition, held 100 years earlier in Hyde Park, the Festival of Britain was a celebration of British design, engineering and manufacturing prowess, and the Festival Hall was a statement of the brave new face of British Architecture, some 6 years after the end of World War Two. The brutalist concrete architecture of the Queen Elizabeth II concert hall and the National Theatre hadn't yet arrived on the South Bank. At other times, mum took us to the annual *Daily Mail Ideal Home Exhibition*, which was staged at the Olympia exhibition centre in Earls Court, though we might have gone with a coach party from the Ufford Women's Institute.

During our schooldays, mum always endeavoured to work hours that allowed her to back home before tea-time, and when she moved from her job at the Woodbridge Canning Factory to that of an office-typist at Notcutts Nurseries in Woodbridge, she learnt Pitman's shorthand at night-school in Ipswich so that she would be a proficient shorthand typist. The small portable Imperial typewriter that she bought to practice on proved invaluable for many years to come.

At least some semblance of normal canning-production had resumed after the war, because things were, maybe, slightly different during it: John Moreton tells us that

"To earn extra money, Mum used to bring home huge sacks of unshelled peas still in the pods with leaves on straight from the fields, during the evenings we had to sit and take the peas out and put them into smaller sacks then mum would take them off to the Woodbridge Canning factory. She received 1 shilling a bag (5p), this would go on for days on end and I often did not go to bed until after 11.oopm, I hated it, our hands used to go green, at school lots of us boys had green hands, and we were made to scrub them in cold water,

with a stiff wire brush which cut your hands if you really pushed too hard"

Maybe by 1945 the pea-podding machine had been invented, given that the Canning Factory used to be able to take uncooked desert pears, cut them in half, pack them into cans, fill them with syrup mechanically and send them down the conveyor belt to be sealed mechanically and then cooked at ultra-high temperature before allowing them to cool off and have paper labels pasted on them. And in winter, the factory would buy in a stock of dates from the Middle East, which would be packed in attractive long, round-ended balsa wood date boxes ready to be wrapped and labelled before being sent off to high-end shops in London and elsewhere, using the Turban brand. I think that Mum was good friends with Esmé Read's mum Joan at the time, and they worked together at the Canning Factory. Esmé, who was about my age, was later to attend Farlingaye School with John and myself, and she married locally when she was 18. Another friend of hers at the Canning Factory was Audrey Peck, mother of Gregory Peck, and she also knew Linda Abbott's mother Florence and dad Jack.

Later my mother became a secretary for Culmax, which was started by the *Culmer* family of Highgate, North London and had made pure bristle paint-brushes since before the turn of the eighteenth century. The firm moved to better-suited premises in Woodbridge in the 1920s, thence to Hertford as part of the larger Addis Group of companies in the 1960s, before reverting to independent-company status and moving to its present base in Grantham, Lincolnshire. It may have been Culmax's move to Hertford that prompted her to leave, but whatever the reason, she then worked as a home-help for the Creighton family close to the Culmax factory and offices. Most important for mum was that she had escaped the back-biting and subversion that she had hitherto encountered, and she was at her happiest doing this relatively stress-free work in a good family setting.

As we grew older, John was more into 'church' than me, subsequently being 'confirmed' and dutifully acting as a 'server' during Sunday morning services. He was also a member of the bell-ringing group doing the Sunday morning pre-service peel. I lost interest in both the church services and Sunday school at the Tanner Sisters' house in Lower Street, and instead would go cycling with Brian Danes, who was also a cycling enthusiast. Brian had a 'fixed-gear' bike, which cycling aficionados know is a bike requiring the cyclist to keep pedalling, no matter how steep the hill, and to keep your feet well away from the pedals when going down a steep hill. We used to cycle from Ufford to Lowestoft or Great Yarmouth and back, and would take turns riding the fixed-gear bike. That said, John did join me on some Sunday mornings when we would join up with the Ipswich YHA cycling group led by Derek and Sheila Adams [on their tandem], meeting outside the Cricketers Arms in Electric Avenue, Ipswich, and would go for a long ride through both East- and West Suffolk. And on one Easter weekend we rode out to Whitwell in Hertfordshire, staying overnight at the youth hostel there. Of course, John and I always had the extra 22 or so miles to cover, living out in Ufford. Neither John nor I had even a second-hand Claude Butler cycle frame, but John had bought a mass-produced Phillips racing bike with four *derailleur* gears and narrowish 1 3/8 inch wide tyres, and I had a Hercules sports bike with straight handlebars. So you might say that what we lacked in classic lightweight bicycles we had to make up in physical exertion!

There was a considerable rivalry between the kids in Lower Ufford and those from Ufford Park [as was] and Upper Ufford. So we used to organize football- and cricket matches between the two groups, and the Lower Ufford team included Michael Miller, Roy Foreman, Johnny Miller and me. I seem to remember that the likes of Graham Challis, Alan Boon, Michael Goldsmith, Keith Dawson and Brian Flatman were our opponents.

Mrs. Raven, the school-cook lived, with her husband in School Lane, Ufford, and they had relatives living towards the bottom of Church Lane, a one minute walk for us, a stone's throw from the village hall. Indeed, their back-garden extended virtually up to the ground where our outdoor earthen closet shed was sited, beyond our neighbour Ted Taylor's garden shed and our own, and an extension of land lying immediately behind our cottage. Violet V Raven died in the locality in the March quarter of 1967, aged 69, and Florence E Raven died in Ipswich in the June quarter of 1965, at the age of 67.

Emily Tanner, the Sunday school teacher, was born in Ipswich in 1912, her brother Albert in 1914, and her sister Ethel in 1916. Ethel died in her first year. Basil was born in 1920, Richard in 1924 and Derick in 1926. The Tanner sisters were cricket enthusiasts, so after Sunday-School, and following Sunday lunch at home, John, me and the Miller boys would go with one of the Tanners in her Austin car to watch a cricket match in a neighbouring village. This was one of only a handful of cars in the village in the mid-1950s and this was a treat for us boys. Nevertheless, the clothes washing still had to be done at the weekend, and we hand-washed all the clothes with a bar of Sunlight soap and cold water. We then rinsed the clothes in clean cold water in our galvanized bath, which we used to place on a patch of grass on the allotment just outside our garden gate. Our washing line was tied to the large Ash tree and reached down to the cottage porch. We ironed the clothes with a cast iron clothes-iron heated on the coal-range in the kitchen, or on the primus stove.

Life wasn't without its surprises at home in Ufford, especially in relation to the impact of the weather. The East Coast floods of 1953 are well known, both the village of Ufford and the town of Woodbridge, lying as they did close to the River Deben, were seriously affected. In Ufford, the Lower Street, which extends down from the village Post Office/general store to the Lion Inn, and then to the brick bridge over the River Deben and thence, via the village football pitch to the railway level-crossing, then to Eyke and Bromeswell. Between the [White] Lion Inn and the bridge we had the extensive flood-plains, which were partially flooded on a fairly regular basis, even though the river itself was periodically dredged. And in 1953, we had serious flooding which moved up from the regular flood-plain meadows to cover the road and reach the row of cottages which included the Kings' and the Murphys' homes. At that time we had River Boards, which were statutory organizations charged with managing our rivers and their floodplains. They were thus able to exercise power over what could or could not be done on river floodplains, their sole yardstick being the protection of the river and its banks and floodplain areas, especially during times of tidal surges and high water discharges along the valleys. There was an automatic barring of development on flood-plains, and that was just as well for Ufford during the 1953 North Sea tidal surge. The North Sea flood of 1953 was one of the most devastating natural disasters ever recorded in the UK. A combination of a high and a severe European wind-storm over the North Sea caused a high spring tide of the North Sea; the combination of wind, high tide, and low pressure led to a water level of more than 5.6 metres (18.4 ft.) above mean sea level in some locations. The flood and waves overwhelmed sea- defences and caused extensive flooding. Over 1,600 km of coastline was damaged, and sea walls were breached, inundating 1,000 km² Having already wreaked enormous damage as well as loss of life on the East Coast of Scotland, the surge raced down the East Coast into the southern North Sea, where it was exaggerated by the shallower waters. In Lincolnshire, flooding occurred from Mablethorpe to Skegness, reaching as far as 2 miles inland. In individual incidents, 38 died at Felixstowe in Suffolk when wooden prefabricated homes in the West End area of the town were flooded. In Essex, Canvey Island was inundated, with the loss of 58 lives. Another 37 died when the seafront village of Jaywick near Clacton was flooded. Reis Leeming, a US airman, was awarded the George Medal for his bravery in rescuing 27 people in the South Beach area of Hunstanton.

Apart from the floods in lower Ufford, I also remember how the River Deben burst its banks in and around Woodbridge, flooding an extensive area of quayside and the Woodbridge Cinema, on the town-side of the railway footbridge. The promenade alongside the river, along with the large model yacht pond were also inundated, and the flood water would have affected the Woodbridge Canning Factory, where mum used to work, because this lay behind the cinema and was at about the same level.

The River Deben, rising beyond Debenham to the north, flows south-east past Ufford to Sutton, Woodbridge, Waldringfield and then the sea.

At Woodbridge, the river is already tidal, forming a salt-water estuary that in earlier centuries had allowed the town to function as a port with its mill and a centre for ship-building on the River Deben. In fact, the tidal estuary of the Deben reaches up to Ufford Mill, near Old Melton Church, where my dad is buried. The churchyard borders on the house where the Sandemans [of port fame] lived later in their lives. The Mill House was far enough from the centres of Ufford and Melton that we only went passed its gates when cycling to Melton along the back road, and I guess this isolation suited the Sandemans, allowing them to truly keep themselves to themselves.

The connection between the Sandemans and Ufford proved quite elusive to check out, but eventually, and to my relief, I traced a reference to the Hon. Mrs. Phyllis Elinor Sandeman [née Legh], living at the Mill House, Melton, near Woodbridge as of April 1954. Mrs. Sandeman was born in London on 9th December, 1895, the daughter of Thomas Wodehouse **Legh,** 2nd Baron Newton and Evelyn Caroline **Bromley Davenport**. The Hon. Mrs. Sandeman grew up on the Lyme Park Estate in Cheshire [now a National Trust property], and wrote `Treasure on Earth: an account of Christmas in an Edwardian Country House." In the book, Phyllis Sandeman recalls the celebrations, the theatricals, the relationships between family and servants and her own childhood hopes and fears. She married Henry Gerard Walter Sandeman, son of Walter Albert Sandeman, in St Georges Hospital Square, near Hyde Park Corner on 31st January, 1918 and lived with her late husband in nearby Belgrave Square, virtually around the corner from Pimlico Square, where I was to work in 1975. Mr. Sandeman later moved with his wife to the Old Mill House, Melton and died 19th January, 1953. He gained the rank of officer in the service of the Grenadier Guards.

The Sandemans had one child, Chloë Sandeman, who married Frederick de la Pole Kenworthy on 18th March, 1948. The couple divorced in 1965. Their children are Forflissa Viola Kenworthy, b. 23.09.1949, Nicolette Elizabeth Kenworthy, b. 14.08.1950 and Emma Yseult Kenworthy, b. 28.02.1958. Forflissa married William John Healey and were living at Whydown, Bexhill in East Sussex in the early 2000s. They have one son and three daughters.

In 1954, Mrs. Sandeman was a member of Suffolk Institute of Archeology, and the list of talks that were given at the Institute is fascinating! She died in 1986 and was buried in the same cemetery at Old Melton Church as my dad, and but a stone's throw from her home. A painting of Mrs. Sandeman, painted with oil-paints on canvas, measuring 59.5 cm x 49 cm and entitled THE HON PHYLLIS ELINOR LEGH, MRS SANDEMAN: An early 20th century painting (1912) by the so-called British School, is on display at Lyme Park (Mrs. Sandemans' childhood home and now a National Trust property in Cheshire].

In the process of checking-out the Sandeman family, I also unearthed a reference to Miss Nancy Churchman, of the Lodge, Melton, near Woodbridge, also a member of the said Institute in that year. Whilst my family had no connection with the Churchmans, we cycled past their estate on our way to and from school and college thousands of times, and the tall brick wall surrounding their home was a sure indication that they were a cut above the likes of our family!

Those readers, who are connoisseurs of the older cigarette and cigar brand names, will recognise Churchman's, whose production was based at Ipswich, where the company sponsored a stand at the Portman Road football stadium of Ipswich Town. The Churchmans' estate extended up the hill from Melton, and John and I followed its tall brick walls as we cycled up the hill towards the Phylis Memorial Maternity Home, where we would turn off to the right and head down past Sheepshanks' Decoy Farm towards Old Melton Church, the adjacent gate to Ufford Mill, and thence Ufford. When I cycled home alone from the scouts in Melton, I was keen to go as fast as I could because it was scary with no street lights on Lower Road, it was pitch black, and I proudly remember the huge light beam generated by my bike's dynamo as I came down the hill at 30+ mph.

And, finally, here's just a bit more on the Churchmans of Melton. Firstly, their house was auctioned in the late 1990s together with its contents; secondly, the Phyllis Memorial nursing home, which was a maternity home for mothers in the Woodbridge area until the 1990s, was funded by Mr Churchman in memory of the daughter who died in childbirth; and thirdly, the road in Melton where my dad spent his last days was Churchman Close. My brother John has informed me [more than forty years later] that he used to work as a part-time jobbing gardener at the nursing home, but was eventually dismissed on account of his poor time-keeping! I doubt very much that he ever repeated that from that time onwards!

Ufford Mill, being the lowest part of the Deben as a freshwater river, was the limit to which my mate and I used to walk from the bridge when we went fishing for eel and pike. Mum wasn't too keen on the idea of my fishing, but she consented and on one occasion we went fishing late at night, because this was apparently the best time to catch the fish. I did not have any fishing tackle myself, but I used to share manning the rod and line with my friend and used to help him to attach the bait to the hooks and to weigh the catch. If the fish were small, we would simply return them painless back into the river. I don't remember taking any of the catch back home for mum to cook, but memory plays funny tricks. Mum was pretty tolerant about most things that John and I wanted to do as kids, but she certainly wasn't happy that my friend Bernard Walton had been given a Diana 0,22 air rifle as a birthday-present by his father, and allowed to shoot down birds with it. I discussed this issue with my mum, and subsequently stopped playing alongside him in what was left of the woods bordering the old Ufford Park.

Through the centuries, Woodbridge has been involved with ship and boat building and as long ago as the 17th century substantial ships were being built here, mainly to transport timber. There was great demand for oak from the Suffolk forests and trading ships were constructed in Woodbridge to carry this valuable cargo. From 1630 to the end of the century 15 *men-of-war* were launched here and there was plenty of work for the town's shipwrights.

During the 18th and 19th centuries, ship-building continued at Lime Kiln Quay and by the mid-19th century Woodbridge could have been called a sailing ship town, with schooners being built and repaired and sail makers, rope and twine makers at work on the Common Quay.

The arrival of the railway and improvements in road transport brought about the end of the town's usefulness as a significant port. The shallow-draft sailing barges which brought coal up the Deben to Sun Wharf unloaded their last cargo in about 1923. The Deben Yacht Club was founded in 1830 and by 1872 the Grand Woodbridge Regatta became an important annual event. A new era of yacht building began in the town when Ebenezer Robertson took over the Lime Kiln Yard in 1884. As yachting flourished on the Deben there was more work for yacht builders and in 1926 Claude Whisstock, a former apprentice with Robertson's yard, opened his own boatyard, which became one of the best known boat builders in Woodbridge and on the East Coast. In 1932 the first sizeable craft was built by Whisstocks – the motor cruiser 'Bendor'. The first Deben 4-tonner was launched in 1937, designed by William Maxwell Blake, a Londoner, and a further 55 were built over the next couple of decades. A one-off design by Blake built by the yard was the 'Florence Edith', which was bought after the war by Sir Francis Chichester and re-named 'Gipsy Moth'. David Blake, who lived in our neighbouring village of Melton, was four or so years my brother's senior, and was a senior scout in the Melton scout group when John and I joined the group.

I remember the name of William Whisstock, a year my senior, who was born in Ipswich in the June quarter of 1944, the place of birth probably being the hospital, given that 1944 was still a time of war. Then there was Fred Whisstock, whose death [registered in the old Samford District] at the relatively young age of 58 in the June quarter of 1957 must have been recorded in the local newspapers at the time, due to the family's connection with the boat-building legacy in Woodbridge. The Samford Registration District included large chunks of the Deben area around Waldringfield, stretching to the Orwell estuary around Ipswich. Harry Whisstock [Fred's dad?] died in 1952 at the age of 79. I was pleased, nevertheless, to see that Whisstocks were still trading on the quayside when we drove past in February 2015.

The riverside at Woodbridge in the 1950s and early 60s owed its charm and its serenity to the fact that it was relatively unspoilt, and I remember the times when mum used to hire a sailing dinghy, and with John and I on board, she would row us along and across the river for next to no cost. And I vaguely recollect that both mum and dad and John and I used to take a model boat which dad had made from kit form and sail it across the model yacht pond next to the riverside promenade.

John Moreton was a Woodbridge kid during the War and loved the ability to explore the Deben riverside and all that it offered kids with no money but plenty of energy and time. He wrote that

"When the tide was low in the river Deben we would take our pritch. (A metal rod with a barbed end, which we use to get from the local blacksmith for just a few pence) then walk around in the mud, feeling underfoot for flatfish. When we felt them wriggle we would spear them with our pritch, spearing ones foot was an occupational hazard, which I managed twice. But as Mother could not afford Doctors fees, we just got on with it; I guess all that mud and salt water helped the healing? Our fish were taken home, and my Gran would soak them in water for a couple of days to remove the muddy flavour before cooking them. Those long summer days during 1940/1, looking back, were very happy and we would wander miles, often finding a field of carrots, fruit, etc., we would steal a handful run like hell, and then eat them. Sugerbeet was a firm favourite, not very tasty but filling...."

4 LOCAL EMPLOYMENT, COMMUNITY INVOLVEMENT AND HIGH SCHOOL MATTERS

Mum was a brilliant linguist who had been born in Austria but had come to England to settle as a young lady. This was the sum total of my knowledge of my late mother's background, and she did not feel the need to elaborate. In Ufford, she volunteered to teach Mrs. Jenvy's daughter Peggy some German, and she taught German at an evening class at Ipswich Technical College, which became Ipswich Civic College. Later, she was to enter herself for the Institute of Linguists' exams, in which she gained Merits and Distinctions.

Mum would on occasion point out The Red House, 44 Cumberland Street, Woodbridge, when our bus to Ipswich passed by it, and she had affectionate memories of its occupants at the time, who were Sir Ian Jacob and his wife, Lady Jacob.

Lt.Gen. Sir Edward Ian Claud Jacob, [1899-1993], to give him his full title, was a professional soldier, serving as Military Assistant Secretary to the British War Cabinet. In 1946 the BBC asked him to run the European Service. He went on to manage all Overseas Services, then took a sabbatical at the Ministry of Defence in 1951. In 1952 he returned as Director-General, a position he held until 1959. Given that Mum had worked for BBC Monitoring during the Second World War, she naturally felt some affinity with the guy who had taken over the reins of 'the Beeb', was popular with its staff, and who lived so close to us. Ian Jacob was a much-trusted ally of Winston Churchill, who, as Prime Minister and in the Foreign

Office, confided in him on numerous occasions. Jacob, perhaps taking his cue from Churchill and his wartime Cabinet politics, was not one to be bullied by Anthony Eden, Churchill's successor as Prime Minister, over the issue of putting out news and programmes about the Suez Crisis, and the BBC's editorial independence generally, which Eden wanted to stifle. Eden, metaphorically licking his wounds later, sought to gain revenge on Ian Jacob by bringing the BBC to heel, such as by drastically cutting his European Services budget. In 1946, Jacob had taken over the helm of a European Services arm of the BBC which, by the time of VE Day, had reached the zenith of its reputation. From a shaky start it had grown into the largest and most trusted foreign-language radio operation in the world. The temporary staff of continental broadcasters and politicians, British journalists, dons, actors and linguists of all kinds assembled at Bush House was a remarkable aggregation of talent, and under Jacob's direction immediately after the War, survived to live another day, successfully reducing the punitive measures which Anthony Eden had sought to impose on the Corporation. Readers might wonder how many of the talented Bush House staff had also worked at BBC Monitoring in Caversham Park during the War. Sir Ian Jacob died in Woodbridge on 24th April, 1993.

John and I had been brought up as church-goers at the local St Mary's Anglican Church, where John was later 'confirmed.' Mum did not attend church, but she encouraged us to go, as well as to attend Sunday school after the morning service. After all, John and I had been christened in Kesgrave church when we first arrived in Suffolk, and, as far as we believed, it was the customary thing for families to do. At the time I had no reason to ponder as to why we were otherwise encouraged to go to church.

As a family, we were outsiders when we moved to Ufford, in the heart of rural England, only slowly becoming accepted as locals. And I guess that Mum was conscious of her very slight `German' accent, especially since Britain had just emerged from a bitter, extended and costly war against Germany. Mum would have been asked countless times during her working day where she came from, though I guess that in the fullness of time, it was not of too much consequence for her, since she had built her own support-system. First, there were the Jenvy's, our near-neighbour, good, solid people who were genuinely kind and helpful. We only knew Mrs. Jenvey and her daughter Peggy, because Mr. Ernest Jenvey had died shortly before we arrived in Ufford. The Jenveys lived in the lower half of the pair of semi-detached cottages just past the gate to our cottage from Church Lane, and our drinking water well was in their garden. Then there was Mrs. King, who lived in a cottage opposite the Lion Inn on the Eyke Road in Lower Ufford. Her daughter had married and migrated to Australia sometime in the 50s, and Mrs. King, who was a seamstress, always happily agreed to turn our shirt-collars when they had become too worn to be acceptable, not to mention the alterations to all our clothes. Next door to Mrs. King was the Murphy family, Mr. Murphy being a painter and decorator and their daughter being Maureen. Then there were the Easty's and the Birts.

I do know that Mum used to attend some of the monthly meetings of the Ufford Women's Institute, which would have been held in the Village Hall at the bottom of Church Lane, where we lived. I believe that she must have been a member in the 1950s, as I don't recollect her going to these meetings in the 1960s, which was the time that she used to travel to Ipswich in the evening to attend shorthand lessons and, later, to teach German conversation.

I recognise all the names of the ladies who, according to the minutes of their meetings held in the Suffolk County Archives, attended the Ufford WI monthly meetings between 1951 and 1956, and can place the homes of most of them in my mental map of the village at that time:

Jenvey, Bradley, Easty, Raven, Leonard, Miller, Evans, Taylor, Birt, Murphy, Potter, Jenkinson, Ling, Woodhouse, Pearce, Corbett, English, Fisk, Dredge, Keeble, Read, Hollicks, Morris, Imrie, Harrison, Booth, Murrell, Tanner, Clements, Johns.

Most of the people that are included in the above list will either have been referred to earlier in my story or will be mentioned later. Of the others, Mrs. Imrie was the wife of Dr. Imrie, who, I believe, wasn't a GP but worked in the school-pupils' health field of medicine. The Imries, who had a daughter and a son [Ian] lived a short distance along the Old Melton Road from the farm where childhood playmate Roy Taylor's dad was the dairyman, and which itself was a little way up from the pair of semi-detached houses occupied by the Miller and Taylor families. And Mrs. Johns was the wife of Father Johns, the village's Anglican rector at the time, and Mrs. Corbett lived at the bottom of Church Lane.

The County Archives then went on to record:

`The meetings always commenced at 7. 30 in the evening, the members would sing Jerusalem, and then followed by the minutes being read out from the previous month's meeting.*

Meetings were held every month except August. There would be guest speakers on occasions coming from different places from around the county of Suffolk, from different businesses, and organizations, one of which was mentioned as being somebody who gave a very interesting talk on living at Bentwaters, with the American servicemen and their families. [Bentwaters was the USAF air-base which was particularly active during the Cold War, and could be reached either from the road linking Melton, Sutton and Hollesley [where novelist-cum-disgraced politician Geoffrey Archer was later to serve his time in the open prison] or along the road from lower Ufford which crossed the river and the railway line and went to the adjoining villages of Bromeswell and Eyke. Fighter-jets from

Bentwaters would fly low over our cottage at all times of the day and night. Kids from Ufford would be invited to go to Bentwaters at Halloween and be treated to donuts and Coca Cola by host American Servicemen's' families.]

Throughout the year, at each month's meetings there would be competitions, outings, handicraft, jam making, cakes, social events and half-hour quizzes. Meetings would be end with the national anthem being sung. I distinctly remember how, on one Halloween, John and I, along with other kids from Ufford, were picked up from home by an American Airforceman's family in their 'Cadillac', enjoyed a pleasant evening at our hosts with loads of Coke and Jonuts, and were then safety taken home.

Our immediate neighbours throughout the time that I lived in Church Lane, Ufford were Ted and Violet Taylor. We got on with the Taylors, and my dad used to enjoy a 'tipple' and a natter with them, especially around Christmas time. The couple was a generation older than our parents, and for the most part, kept themselves to themselves. Ted was the village roadman until retirement, and his wife was a housewife. He would be seen out clearing the snow from the village roads early in the mornings during the cold winters that we experienced when I was a child. The Taylors had no children and Violet was scarcely if ever seen around the village. They displayed a great deal of patience as far as my brother and I and our friends were concerned, especially when we were younger and our football had to be retrieved from their garden. Eventually we concurred with mum's plea that we played football on the lane or on the meadow, rather than on our lawn. Ted died in the December quarter of 1965, aged 67, and I believe that at that point his wife Violet was transferred to a residential home. She died in Ipswich in the March quarter of 1969, aged 79. I shall always remember how Violet's brother, who lived in a nearby village, tried for 'countless times' over many years to pass his driving test, and when eventually he did gain his driving license, he called round to collect Ted and Violet and take them out for a drive in his new car, which I seem to recollect was a black Ford Popular.

In this connection, I was delighted to come across an Ufford Church marriage record dated 8th December, 1845, for the groom, a **James Noy** of Ufford, *Roadman and Widower*, and the bride, an **Anne Gillings**, also of Ufford and described as a *Servant and Spinster*! Ted was not a clock-watcher, but someone who relied on his own initiative to decide what he needed to do on the lower village roads and footpaths, depending on the season of the year and the weather. It seems that in so doing, he was carrying on in the tradition of his predecessors!

Ted Taylor was the village roadman until retirement, and his wife was a housewife. He would be seen out clearing the snow from the village roads early in the mornings during the cold winters that we experienced when I was a child. The Taylors had no children and Violet was scarcely if ever seen around the village. They displayed a great deal of patience as far as my brother and I and our friends were concerned, especially when we were younger and our football had to be retrieved from their garden. Eventually we concurred with mum's plea that we played football on the lane or on the meadow, rather than on our lawn. Ted died in the December quarter of 1965, aged 67, and I believe that at that point his wife Violet was transferred to a residential home. She died in Ipswich in the March quarter of 1969, aged 79. I shall always remember how Violet's brother, who lived in a nearby village, tried for 'countless times' over many years to pass his driving test, and when eventually he did gain his driving license, he called round to collect Ted and Violet and take them out for a drive in his new car, which I seem to recollect was a black Ford Popular.

Frank Rush and his wife Jessie lived in what was probably the largest detached house in Church Lane, virtually across the road from us, and had a daughter Daphne, the older child, and a son called Anthony [C], who was born in the June quarter of 1940. Jack worked for the Post Office, erecting telephone poles and aerial telephone cables. This was when the Post Office not only collected and delivered mail throughout the UK, but also provided and maintained the [nationalized] telephone network throughout the country. Daphne married into the Double family of Ipswich in the September quarter of 1953. Sally Jane Double was born in Ipswich in the March quarter of 1971.

Frank Rush's older brother Jack, along with his wife Elsie May [née Youngman] and their only son Johnny, lived in a semi-detached cottage near the bottom of Church Lane. Elsie was born in 1899, and her birth was registered in the *Plomesgate* District of Suffolk, with its sub-districts being Aldburgh, Earl Soham, Framlingham, Orford, Saxmundham and Wickham Market. This potential registration district name for Elsie's birth flummoxed me for a moment, but it soon became clear that, with the inclusion of Wickham Market, itself just two to three miles to the north of Ufford, this was perfectly plausible for the year 1899. The new Deben registration district, along with those of Blyth and Hartismere, replaced Plomesgate in April 1935.

Johnny was some three or so years older than my brother John, and was not deemed able to gain conventional employment, but we regarded him as one of our peer-group when it came to playing football on the meadow down Church Lane, past the Rectory. Johnny always gave me a helping hand clearing and managing our part of the allotment outside the cottage gate. He never shirked at helping me clear the stinging nettles from an unclaimed part of the allotment beyond our own, to bring it back into cultivation, and we loved gathering the harvest of Bramley apples from that part of the allotment in autumn. Johnny enjoyed partaking of a peanut butter sandwich and a mug of milk after the hard-graft on the allotment had been accomplished. Friday was a special day of every week for Johnny and his parents, because it was the day when Elsie made Toad-in-the-hole [batter with sausages] for lunch, and once or twice I would be invited to share this meal with them. I always regarded this as a real privilege, especially since the family was very poor and struggled to make ends meet. Elsie May Rush died in Ipswich in the December quarter of 1964, at the age of 65, leaving Jack and Johnny to cope at home. Jack H. Rush died at home in the September quarter of 1967, aged 73, with the consequence that Johnny was placed in a safe residence from that point onwards.

I did not fully understand what an extended family was, when I was a child, so I didn't think about it and therefore didn't yearn for it. Whilst we had been guests at Uncle Alf's when I was a mere baby, Alf's family did not really figure in our childhood, and the rest of my dad's family (his sister Alice and four of the five surviving brothers), were miles away in the North-East of England or in Derbyshire. Besides, mum preferred to take John and myself out on her own, and her very limited budget tested her ingenuity. All my friends' families were in the same boat, so to speak, especially in the decade following the end of the Second World War, so it was not embarrassing to ask for groceries to be 'put on the slate' when we needed some food from the local post office and store. George Evans, the sub-postmaster/shop-owner/local postman whom John and I used to refer to affectionately as 'Jidge', must have trusted us to pay him at the end of any week, when people had been paid, otherwise he wouldn't have granted the credit in the first place! George, who delivered the post in our part of the village before opening up shop in the morning, had sold up the post office and village shop a while before mum and I left for London, and was succeeded by Bill Walker and his wife. George died in 1957 at the age of 62.

In several of our school summer holidays, mum would buy a family rail ticket for one week, which allowed us to travel without restriction within the East of England rail zone. This meant that we could go on day-trips to the seaside at Yarmouth, Lowestoft, Clacton, and, maybe, Southend. We tried to spot Roy Hudd at the seaside, since the *News Chronicle* national daily newspaper offered prizes for finding him!

This railway travel concession was heaven-sent for families such as ours, especially since so few people could afford to own cars, and coach-travel was not really a universal means of travel. I remember that we had a Grey- Green coach that ran from Ipswich to London (Stamford Hill), and this was run by George Ewer, but these were before the days of National Express Coaches. We probably took the coach to London and back once or twice, but it was still regarded as a luxury. Actually, Grey-Green can trace its origins back over a century to the foundation of George Ewer's horse carriage business in 1885. The first service to operate throughout the year was a London to Ipswich service that commenced in June 1928, and it seems incredible that the Arriva buses that we see across the country owe their origin, in part on their Grey-Green forebears!

In 1919, two entrepreneurs named Wolsey, using a fleet of motor-buses, put together in rural Suffolk a network of passenger routes. Regulation in 1931 led four operators to amalgamate to serve all East Anglia. Then, in the years after 1945, `Eastern Counties` was wholly owned by government. Its growth was first checked by rising private-car ownership, and then encouraged by rail closures. Loss-making services withdrawn in 1968 on nationalisation were only partly replaced by independent operators. The new county councils were given powers to provide financial support. Then in 1984/5 began a process of de-nationalising and de-regulating, and the mini-bus became popular. Publicly-funded support to meet social need replaced both unregulated competition and near-monopoly.

The other highlight – for me, at least – was the trip to Aldeburgh in the summer holidays, when I was sometimes invited to accompany my friends in the Miller family when they went to stay with Aunt in Aldeburgh for a few days. One of the fascinations for us boys was roaming the shingle beach and looking for shells. The trip generally coincided with the staging of the Aldeburgh Festival, so there were lots of visitors arriving to hear performances of the music of Benjamin Britten and Peter Piers and others. Britten lived fairly close to the sea-front at the time, but I would not have recognised him anyhow! And this was before the Snape Maltings had been converted into a concert hall for the Aldeburgh Festival. Mark and Beatrice Miller [née Finch] and their family lived just around the corner from the village post-office in Ufford, in a semi-detached house set down a drive from the Old Melton Road. Mark drove cattle trucks for Carters, and Beatty stayed at home to look after the children, Richard, Janet, John, Michael and Peter. Richard [known to us as Dickie] was born in the March quarter of 1939 and Janet was born in the September quarter of 1942. Richard was called up for National Service in the late 1950s before compulsory conscription was abolished. And then there was Auntie Marjorie, another of the Miller family, who worked as a hostess on the Queen Mary ocean liner, which sailed between Southampton and New York, and there was a buzz of excitement when she came home on leave because she was regarded as having quite a glamorous job. Peter, the youngest member of the family, eventually became a bus driver with London Transport.

I recollect that mum took us to visit [and maybe stay over at] at a house on the Essex coast which was built as a Martello tower for coastal rebuttal of enemy fire many years ago, and converted into a private residence more recently. The owners may have been friends of the Filtness family from London, who we were friends of.

The Essex- and South- coasts have always been vulnerable to attack from the seaward side, as was the case during the Napoleonic period [1791-1815]. A chain of defensive fortresses, large cylindrical structures , maybe ten or so metres in height and known as Martello Towers, was built to defend the coastal towns from Napoleon's forces. The threat of invasion, or at least, coastal naval action by the French navy, prompted the building of these Towers along the south coast, followed by the east coast, the latter having towers stretching from Point Clear near St Osyth in Essex, to Aldeburgh/Slaghden in Suffolk. Of the 29 towers built on the East Coast, 18 survive. Inside each of the towers there were two main floors, the lower floor housing supplies and a powder store.

For the rest, Mum had bought us a *Mobo* scooter, and we kids spent many hours racing up and down our lane on this scooter, not always with the blessing of Mrs. Barker, who lived in the thatched cottage opposite our allotment gate onto Church Lane. For many years after, this type of scooter seemed to have gone out of fashion, but now it seems to have become popular once more. The year 1956 was a critical year for both my brother and me, because we both started at Farlingaye Secondary Modern School in Woodbridge. When we started, my mother recognised that we would both need a bicycle, since the new school was located at the far end of Woodbridge, and was simplest to reach via the back roads and the [then] Woodbridge bypass. Besides which, we much preferred buying ha'penny chews to paying bus fares!

The school had only been open for a year before we joined, and initially we were the only pupils from Ufford, which fell within the Wickham Market Area School catchment area. Mum had to overcome 'red-tape' to facilitate this move and a certain Mr Bevan of Ransome Road, Woodbridge was the benevolent facilitator. Mr Bevan was an elderly grocer working at Gobbitt and Kirby's the Grocers in the Thoro'fare in Woodbridge, where mum did some of her shopping. Mum figured that if my brother and I had an address in Woodbridge, then the local education authority could not object to our attending Farlingaye School. So John and I used to spend three or so nights as 'lodgers' at Mr Bevan's bungalow close by to the school, only leaving once we had become 'accepted' as pupils at the school.

The headmaster at the time, Mr Ted Savage, somewhat tacitly – but with good humour – accepted that it was unreasonable to bar us from the school even when we had reverted to living full-time at home in Ufford, although it would be another 2-3 years before Ufford became part of the Farlingaye School catchment area. Today, Farlingaye High School is a mixed comprehensive school for pupils 11-18. The main school has 1,418 pupils on its roll and a further 326 in the sixth form. This is a far cry from the 500-odd pupils who were at the school when it was in its infancy, and, who, until it began to offer GCE Ordinary Level teaching in 1960, ran a four-year curriculum and had four streams in each year. Mr. Freeman, my math's teacher and form tutor, was a big tease, and gave me a lot of stick on Monday mornings if my favourite football team had lost at the weekend. Can you imagine his delight therefore when my idols - then playing in Division One as the top division - were beaten 3-0 in the third round of the FA cup by a fairly local team who were only in Division Three South. This was an embarrassing Giant Killing, good and proper! And just to prove how serious I and most of my class-mates were about the 'beautiful game', and how partisan we were, we sported the team-shirt of the different teams we supported when we had football as our sports lesson at school; and my school classmate David J. Leech and I used to take the train to Norwich in the 'close-season' to watch the professional players of Norwich City practice at their Carrow Road ground in readiness for the new season, and would be invited to join in the kickabouts. David, like me, was born in early summer of 1945, and had a brother called Neville, five years his senior. My mother would have known members of the local Rattle family, which included David's mum. And of course there was Jon Sammels a fellow classmate, who was undoubtedly the most talented footballer in the school, representing the county of East Suffolk and England Schoolboys in the game. I remember that on one occasion I lent Jonny my Adidas football boots for a representative match. Jonny joined the village football team of Westerfield when he was still at school, by which time he had been talent-spotted by Arsenal, his favourite team, and he was soon to join the Arsenal as a youth player when he left school. Jonny, like classmates Neville Rayment, Richard Quinton and Michael Mayhew, hailed from Grundisburgh, and had an incredibly powerful shot, even with a `dead ball', and he could make mincemeat out of all defenders who faced him. In fact Jonny was also a talented cricketer who played for his county in the game. Jonny has a brother called Richard, a year older than him. Another two gifted footballers in my class were Vincent Addison [`Vinnie"] and Terry [`Beans'] Bennett, who has an older brother Anthony. I believe that Terry was considering training as a merchant-navy chef when he left school. Anyhow, he married in Flintshire in North Wales, in late 1962. Neville Rayment has a younger brother called David. Peter Wright, the older son of the Wright family, which ran the patisserie in the Thorofare in Woodbridge, was also in my year, and he had a younger brother, Keith. Amongst the girls in my class were Linda Drew, Sylvia Miller, Esmé Read, Anne Hill and Beryl Neale. Sylvia married in 1964 and Beryl married in the March quarter of 1968. Beryl's first child, Philip David, was born a year later, and Stuart John was born in 1972. In my third and penultimate year at Farliingaye School, my brother and I invited Jimmy Gant – who lived on the estate at the back of the school playing field and was another football enthusiast – to join us on an extended weekend in London, staying at one of the youth hostels and going along to watch games at Highbury [Arsenal], Upton Park [West Ham United] and Craven Cottage [Fulham] on Good

Friday, Easter Saturday and Easter Monday. In those days, kids could get into the football ground quite cheaply, and we watched from the terraces in those days. Jimmy was nearly two years my junior but used to join me and my classmates playing kickabouts on the school playground.

Mum's was a very familiar face in Woodbridge town centre, since she had shopped there for years. It was therefore quite easy for her to persuade the Hasnip brothers – who owned a cycle shop in the Thoro'fare and then one in Wickham Market - to offer her hire-purchase terms for two new Hercules cycles. John and I were thenceforth able to exploit the freedom which these bikes offered. Meanwhile, Mum always walked the mile each way from home to the bus stop next to the Crown public house, and all around the town centre in Woodbridge. Mum and I used to catch the 8.05am Service 203 bus from Ufford Crown in the morning, when I had started at Ipswich Civic College, and I cycled up to the bus stop because I would leave the bike in Mrs. Booth's garden next to the bus stop, and pick it up when I came home in the evening. Mum would take the short cut on the path across the farmer's field [which later became Dougie Goldsmith's nursery field] which led to the main road above the bus stop, and many were the times when mum was on the late side and hadn't reached the top of the path before the bus had left Ufford Crown and was climbing up the road past the top of the path. Happily the bus driver would predict that mum was approaching the top of the path, and would stop just there and wait a couple of minutes to let mum reach the top of the path and, breathless by now, clamber on the bus! After all, the next bus wasn't due for another 30 minutes and mum needed to do her shopping in Woodbridge before she started work. And if I was late leaving home, I would listen out for the bus as I raced along School Lane towards the main road, because we could hear the unmistakable chugging of its engine over half a mile away, near Pettistree. There were even occasions when I didn't have time to put my bike in the small shed in Mrs. Booth's garden, and had to leave it propped against the garden fence, under the walnut tree. Our family was therefore indebted to Mrs. Booth, another one of Mum's trusted friends, who only charged us about 2 old pence a day for leaving our bikes there. Those were civilized times when I had a free bus pass which allowed me to take the bus to Ipswich and back not only on the five weekdays but also on the Saturday morning when I played football for the college team.

Cousin Stan, who was our Aunt Alice's son, did come to visit us one year, and this was a special occasion, especially for my dad, since Stan brought news of the family on Tyneside. At the time, Stan was working on a civil engineering project on the railway in London, and, out of the blue, decided to take the train out to Ipswich to visit us. Was dad pleased that day when Stan showed up! Dad's brother Alf was, unbeknown to John and myself, going through a difficult time at home, and Albert, yet another of Dad's brothers who had moved to near Ipswich, was struggling with alcohol.

5 THROUGH SCHOOL TO COLLEGE AND WORKING LIFE

Wilhelm Wolf was a friend of my mum who she invited round one day. Wilhelm was a young German horticulturalist who had come to work for a spell at Notcutt's Nurseries in Woodbridge. John Dyter was, I believe, the Sales Director of the firm at the time. My mother was fluent in German, since it was her 'mother tongue', and so she could chat to Wilhelm about Germany, etc., in their shared language.

John and I joined the Melton Boy Scout group at about the time that I started secondary modern school, and we spent many enjoyable evenings and weekends with our scout-troop friends such as Nigel Clark ['Nidg'], under the watchful eye of Jack Cook and his wife Elsie. At the time, Jack was a car-mechanic with *Fairhead and Sawyer*, a company which had a garage between Melton and Woodbridge. Weekend camping expeditions to Foxboro' Hall, near Melton, were one of the highlights of scout-life at Melton, as were the annual scout jamborees, such as Sandringham Park in Norfolk and Sutton Park near Sutton Coalfield in Warwickshire. This **World Scout Jubilee Jamboree** at Sutton Park was from the 1st to the 12th August 1957, and scouts from 85 countries converged on the Park to celebrate 50 years of scouting and the centenary of Lord Baden-Powell's birth. One thing that could not be catered for was the weather and a huge storm on the night of the 5th August, with an inch of rain falling in less than an hour, flooded out around 1,000 scouts. Most were quickly moved to other tents but some were taken in by local residents, which led to lifelong friendships being formed. I had no idea at the time that the first children born to my dad's parents were George Baden-Powell and Martin Kitchener, twins who were to die within months of being born.

Mum even volunteered to organise scout-troop visits to the printing press of the *East Anglian Daily Times* newspaper in Ipswich and to WS Cowell's printing works, in the Buttermarket in Ipswich, both to enrich our knowledge. I believe that Cowell's printed the *Progress* magazine which was published by the Anglo-Dutch food and detergents giant called Unilever, who sent her a free copy every month for years. Cowells the printers had been around for a good many years when we visited their works.

And by 1834, in early Victorian times, three printers had premises in the Buttermarket Ipswich: Stephen Piper (who lived there), the Pawsey/Haddock family and the Cowell family. At the `Ancient House, Frederick Pawsey`s widow, having married his assistant James Haddock, continued his business, followed by her son.

The Cowell family, the largest of Ipswich's printers, was already showing itself to be a progressive firm, and it extended into neighbouring property, adding new buildings and improvements. By 1888, under the first Cowell`s grandson, iron steam-powered machinery replaced hand and treadle operation. Fine results at fast speeds were claimed, using a range of machines for different types of work. Two colours became possible. The increased demand from a more literate society was being met. Our favourite bookshop in Ipswich was the Ancient House, housed in a fine Tudor building in the centre of town, though at the time I had no idea of its roots as a printing firm. Furthermore, Mum was a good friend of the Pawsey's, who lived in Upper Ufford, who were probably descendants of the Pawsey/Haddock printing family, though, again, I had no idea in my youth of the possible local connections of the Pawsey family.

John and I had a German Boy Scout pen-friend at the time called Karl-Heinz Vogler, who lived in Oldenburg. As scouts, we subscribed to an international scouting magazine, and were thus able to become pen- friends with another boy-scout from overseas. We wrote to each other regularly, keeping each other informed of what we were doing in our lives, especially at school and in the boy-scouts.

Mum was outward-looking, and encouraged John and myself to be the same. Although, as a family, we were financially limited as to how far we could travel, mum was keen that John and I went on school-trips to Interlaken in the Bernese Alps in Switzerland and to the Rhine Valley in Germany. This was a huge financial undertaking on my mum's part, and gives an indication of just how important it was for her that we did not grow up being insular and narrow-minded. Mum was also on the mailing list for Unilever quarterly magazine entitled `Progress' and this kept her informed about worldwide progress in the realms of science, medicine, business and culture. At the time there was no internet, and we had neither telephone nor television at home. As a family, we were therefore relatively isolated in the middle of the countryside, and our village had not yet been swallowed up by the London commuter-belt. As teenagers, John and I were encouraged to `spread our wings'. All three of us belonged to the Youth Hostels Association of England and Wales, and John and I were sent on *YHA/Eagle* magazine holidays, to learn sailing at Maldon in Essex, which was fairly close to home, and to learn the rudiments of photography at Wilderhope Manor in the county of Shropshire. Mum had apparently done quite a bit of travelling as a young teenage girl, and was keen for us to be `bitten by the same `travel bug.' She was not overly protective of us as teenage boys and was quite happy for us to join the local YHA cycling group in Ipswich and to disappear for day-long 80+mile cycle jaunts through the Suffolk and Essex countryside. Meanwhile, she would merrily stay at home on periodic weekends, leafing through the latest issues of the *Times Educational Supplement* and *The Lady*, and taking particular interest in articles in *The*

Family Doctor that, at the time, expounded the principles of the likes of Dr. Spock.

School holidays sometimes saw all three of us hitch-hiking at a time when there was next to no hesitation on the part of motorists to stop when hailed-down by a safe-looking hitch-hiker. Unlike me, mum had no compunction and would send John and myself ahead on the road, so that when she had managed to persuade a driver to slow down and stop, we were the first to tell the driver where we were heading for. After all, the most the driver need say was 'Jump in' or 'I'm sorry.'

The first holiday after we had enrolled at Farlingaye School, we set off for North Wales, landing up at Bangor and Betwys-y-coed in Snowdonia. We slept over at the local youth hostels on a self-catering basis and bought provisions at the hostel store and then cooked our meals in the hostellers' kitchen.

I well remember the journey home from Wales, because we were on the A5 Trunk Road outside Llanrwst, near Betwys. Eventually, a car stopped for us and the lone driver asked our destination. We said that we were heading home to East Suffolk, and he kindly agreed to take us as far as London, even though this represented a considerable detour for us, as the crow flies. As usual, mum took the passenger seat at the front of the car, and in the course of conversation with the driver, learnt that he was a good friend of Ted Savage, the headmaster of Farlingaye, our new school in Woodridge, some 77 or so miles away from London. Our chance meeting with the car-driver was an amazing coincidence, and no doubt the driver informed Mr Savage of this, in years to come! And no doubt Mr Savage chuckled to himself!

I had not taken French lessons sufficiently seriously at school, but, when living in London later, came to recognise the importance of having French as a second language. In this I was encouraged by my mother, who had retained basics of the language from her school-days and learnt more alongside me. Neither my brother nor I had learnt German as children, which might seem odd, since it was our mum's native tongue. At the time, mum said that she wanted to bring us up as English children and she later explained that she did not want us to have a muddled sense of identity as children by learning German as well. However, mum did help our near-neighbour Peggy Jenvy with spoken German and had eventually taught the language at Technical College/Civic College evening classes in Ipswich. My mother did not want it to be widely known in our village that she spoke German fluently and was from Austria. Given that Ipswich was 11 miles away, the sense of anonymity this gave her, made teaching German easier for her. When our family first moved to Ufford, the World War 2 had just ended and Germany had been defeated, though at an enormous cost in terms of lives to both the victors and the defeated. It was therefore very understandable that villagers would react suspiciously to anyone living in their midst who spoke German, even though Mum was from Austria. Nevertheless, mum did teach us to sing the carol 'Silent Night' in German at Christmas time, and had immersed herself in German literature modern and older as part of her preparation for the German 'A' level exam. Mum revelled at the opportunity to pour through the writings of Goethe alongside such authors as Hugo von Hofmannsthal, Berthold Brecht, Thomas Mann, Stephan Zweig and Max Frisch. Why then, you might ask, did mum bother about German 'A' level exams when she was fluent in the language and taught it? I guess it was for her a way of gaining academic recognition as a linguist and a rung up the ladder to greater academic achievement, especially in the German language.

Whilst John and I had enjoyed attending Farlingaye Secondary Modern School, and can proudly say that we did not miss a day for the whole of our four years there, there were serious gaps in my education which I soon recognised. If your teacher is enthusiastic about his/her subject, then this will 'rub off' of you, and this was certainly true of Mr Freeman our maths teacher and Mr Wells, our Geography teacher. I can't honestly say that Mr Scopes helped me understand any of the sciences, and I have to thank Dick Alger at the Ipswich Civic College for restoring my faith in science teachers. Mr Alger's favourite teasers were his Americanised spelling of the word `aluminium' and his pronunciation of the last letter of the alphabet as `Zee!'

For John's part, he managed to be accepted as an indentured apprentice at Notcutt's Nurseries in Woodbridge, where mum had work for a while, and gained valuable experience in all aspects of horticulture, including propagation methods and all other nursery practices. One of his valued workmates and mentors was Nathan Pizzey, who was born in 1896 married Ms. Savage in Woodbridge in late 1921 and was approaching retirement age when my brother John was beginning his training. Nathan died in 1993 at the good old age of 96 or 97years. Then there was Charlie Catchpole, another long-serving employee who John also worked alongside whilst at Notcutts. I recollect that John and Charlie used to do a lot of budding and grafting of plants, and I believe that Charlie married in Woodbridge in summer of 1940, after the start of World War Two. John was to spend a year at the former Isle of Ely Horticultural College near Wisbech in the county of Cambridgeshire when he was about 18, and this was funded by the local Education Committee.

In the 1960s and 1970s, Notcutts were one of the leading firms of nurserymen/growers in the country, ranking alongside the likes of Hilliers and the Waterers' Nurseries. Notcutts were expanding quite rapidly in the East of England and the Midlands [I think it was Solihull]. But my brother John would be the first person to tell you that life on a plant nursery could be really tough during a spell of rough weather. Take the winter of 1962/1963: many readers will recall that we experienced some of the most extended freezing weather for decades. Indeed, it was so cold that the ground frost had penetrated many inches and Notcutts were forced to lay-off their nurserymen for weeks. There was simply nothing that these men could do on the ground at that time, whereas in normal winters they would be lifting bare-rooted or balled and burlapped trees and shrubs ready to be dispatched across the country. One commentator recalled that:

".... during 27 December 1962, the cloud steadily thickened and the east wind picked up ...... crisp, clear and frosty weather followed over the next few days .... but the cold went on, and on, until 2 March, 1963! "

For my part, I left Farlingaye School at the age of 15 and, despite a kind and sincere invitation to stay by Headmaster Ted Savage, opted instead to study for my GCE 'O' levels at the Ipswich Civic College. I really did want to be with my peer-group and older people at this point in time!

This was an important year for the College, which had just succeeded its predecessor Ipswich Technical College and was now housed in what in large-part were new buildings. Frank Metcalfe, who had been head of the Engineering School at the erstwhile Technical College, was appointed Principal of the Civic College. By21[st] July 1961, when H.M. The Queen visited the new Ipswich Civic College and was received by Frank Metcalfe, Principal of the College at the time, I had completed the first year of my GCE O level course at the College, and we had probably broken up for summer holidays by then.

Our maths teacher was Charles Whalley, a Lancastrian with a lovely 'tache' who lived in nearby Kesgrave, the same village where my [paternal] uncle Alf, Auntie Nancy and Cousins Sylvia, Sonia and Stella had lived. And then we had Sheila Chapman as our Geography teacher, whose enthusiasm for her subject was infectious. She took us on memorable week-long Field Study trips to the Edale in the Peak District and Robin Hood's Bay on the North Yorkshire Coast. I was therefore saddened to learn of her passing relatively recently, but happy that she was able to spend her last days in the heart of the Suffolk countryside, away from the hustle and bustle of her much-changed home-town of Ipswich.

Our O level group was a talented group of students with a wide variety of family backgrounds: Colin Keeble's dad worked in Ipswich Docks, and I think that Michael Flynn's dad did too. David Isaacs' dad was at Bexford [BX] Plastics in Manningtree, where they made ` *Ilford*' brand black and white photographic roll film. Colin Gilbert was a talented jazz-pianist who could extemporize effortlessly. Michael Johnson was an outstanding ball-room dancer who taught *Victor Sylvester style* dancing at one of the large cinemas in Ipswich every Saturday morning. Brian Clements's dad was a prison officer at Hollesley Bay Borstal Home which later acquired a degree of fame – or was it notoriety? - as the Open Prison where famous author [and discredited politician] Geoffrey Archer served his time. And Brian Miller's dad was a farmer in Peasinghall, a good number miles north of Ufford up the A12 trunk road. Needless to say, Brian, along with Denis Bacon from Halesworth, travelled south to Ipswich by train every weekday morning during term-time, since it was far too far to travel by bus, and, thankfully, they had free season-tickets. Brian Clements, who was proud of his Shrewsbury roots, once organised a football match between the college's `B 'team - which I captained for a while - and a team of borstal boys at Hollesley. Needless to say, we College lads made sure we had our shin pads well secured throughout the match, even though we lost it on that occasion!

There were several O level groups running in parallel at the college, and Terry Parr from Wickham Market, to the north of Ufford, was in a different group to mine. He would travel on the same bus as me in the mornings, and soon after he reached his seventeenth birthday he passed his driving test. On occasion, his surveyor-father would then lend him his *Humber Hawk* car, and Terry would give me a lift to college, proudly demonstrating to me how easy it was for his dad's car to top `the ton' [i.e. exceed 100 miles per hour] on the bypass between Ufford and Martlesham. I think this was before we had the 70 mph speed limit on our roads......!

By the time that my mother had agreed that I could stay on and do GCE A levels, Barry Gooch and Anne Hill, both from Woodbridge and former classmates at Farlingaye School, had decided to join me; and we also had Barry Brown, David Isaacs, Ray Fairweather, Patricia Walker and Valerie Holmes from my GCE O level group. Valerie was a very quiet but quite exceptional student who would most times be buried behind a book in the college library if she was not in a class. Mary Horrocks, a farmer's daughter, was another member of our group, but quite an extrovert! She was a talented organist who, like Ray Fairweather, embarked on teacher-training when she left college. Teacher-training seemed at the time to be the 'default' choice of many fellow-students after completing their A levels, but was not one that I entertained. It is strange how 'wheels go full circle' and that I was to gain my Post-Graduate Certificate in Education many, many years later, after which I began teaching at colleges and at my local university in West Yorkshire.

I was delighted to 'graduate' from the College's soccer 'B' team to a defender in the more-senior Minors soccer team, which included Paul Hayward in goal and Bohdan Jelinski, Colin Keeble and John Ablitt in attack. The team was managed by Stan Smith the College Caretaker, who would be seen attending to his college responsibilities during the week, wearing his khaki cotton coat, but who would turn up at the match venues on Saturday mornings in his beige gabardine raincoat and carrying his small leather suitcase. Inside this suitcase were the oranges which he cut into quarters with his penknife at half-time and distributed among the team. During the week, all team members eagerly watched the notice board in the college foyer, where Stan would pin up his selected team for the coming Saturday's match. Incidentally, John Ablitt married in 1964 and Bohdan Jelinski [known to us as 'Jinx'] married in 1971.

When the weather was warm and sunny, I used to cycle all the way from Ufford to Ipswich [a round- trip of about 22 miles], and, because I rode along the former A12 for much of the journey, I remember having to brace myself for the steep climb up the hill at Martlesham, at the summit of which the road would fork in two directions: Ipswich to the right, via Kesgrave and Rushmere, and Waldringfield and Felixstowe to the left. As I left Martlesham, and to my left, I would skirt the war-time aerodrome of Martlesham Heath, with its miles of runways and its large corrugated metal aircraft-hangers dominating the skyline. And a bit further along the road I would pass the country road to Bealings. Redevelopment of Martlesham Aerodrome was to start before I left for London, and I can distinctly remember that there were some red-and-cream *Eastern Counties* buses to Melton, Ufford and beyond, which took a detour through the new [private] housing estate on the far-side of the former aerodrome at Martlesham Heath before re-joining the main-road. And my brother John has now reminded me that the buses from Ipswich to Ufford and then on to Aldeburgh now travel through the new village on Martlesham Heath. Indeed, when my wife Lynne, my brother John and I drove from Ufford to Ipswich in early 2015, we soon left the original bypass, and had to make a short detour west of Martlesham in order to find this earlier bypass and follow it to Ipswich. Gone was the open vista across the short-grassed wide expanses of the former wartime aerodrome, replaced by images of high-density residential areas partly hidden behind a shallow woodland screen.

Martlesham Heath Aerodrome began life as a Royal Flying Corps [RFC] airfield during the First World War. It then became home to the RFC Aeroplane Experimental Unit in 1917 before the Unit became the Aeroplane and Armament Experimental Station in 1924, testing and evaluating many of the aircraft types, armaments and other equipment that would subsequently be employed during World War Two. No. 15 Squadron, RAF and No. 22 Squadron RAF were based at

Martlesham in the 1920s, and No. 64 Squadron came in the 1930s. At the outbreak of war 9th September, 1939, Martlesham became the most northerly station of No. 11 Group RAF, Fighter Command. Squadrons of Bristol Blenheim bombers, Hawker Hurricanes, Supermarine Spitfires and Hawker Typhoons operated from this airfield, and among the many pilots based there were such famous men as Robert Stanford Tuck, and Squadron-Leader Douglas Bader[of Dam Buster fame], who was based in Martlesham as Commanding Officer of 242 Squadron. Douglas Bader was to lead *Operation Chastise*, which was an attack on German dams carried out on 16–17 May 1943 by Royal Air Force No. 617 Squadron, subsequently publicized in the film `The Dam Busters' (1955). This was a British Second World War film recreating the true story of the air-raid over Germany, starring Michael Redgrave and Richard Todd and directed by Michael Anderson.

In 1943, Martlesham Heath had become one of a group of grass-surfaced airfields earmarked for use by fighters of the United States Army Air-forces (USAAF) Eighth Air Force. The airfield was assigned USAAF designation Station 369. The 356th Fighter Group [FG] served in combat from October 1943, participating in operations that prepared for the invasion of the Continent, supporting the landings in Normandy and the subsequent Allied drive across France and Germany. The Fighter Group was under the command of the 67th Fighter Wing of the VIII Fighter Command. Our dad was part of the Normandy landings, though I don't know whether he was to realize later in life how crucial was the rôle of the RAF and United States Army Air force [USAFF] crews from Martlesham during that landing.

Ian Smith, a fighter pilot and lieutenant in the RAF who was based at Martlesham for part of his war-time service, was later to become the post-war Rhodesian prime minister remembered most for his **Unilateral Declaration of Independence** [UDI] during Harold Wilson's time as Prime Minister of the UK. Ian Smith had initially joined the all-white conservative Rhodesian Front to prevent an immediate shift to black-majority rule in British Colonial Rhodesia in 1961 in protest at the territory's new constitution, and the following year helped Winston Field to form the all-white, firmly conservative Rhodesian Front(RF), which called for the colony's full independence, and was Leader of the Opposition and a stridently vocal critic of Robert Mugabe, during Mugabe's first seven years in power following the international recognition of Zimbabwe's independence in 1980.

For many years, Martlesham Heath remained undeveloped, but the Post Office [predecessor of British Telecom [BT]] began work on the Martlesham Heath Post Office Laboratories around 1968, and these were completed in 1971. Most if not all the building design work for the Post Office in the 1960s was undertaken by the former Ministry of Public Building and Works [MPBW] and Martlesham was no exception, the complex being named Adastral Park. This development became the Post Office/BT's main information and communications technology research facility in the UK, now employing around 4000 research and development staff.

I became involved with design work for the Post Office/ MPBW whilst studying in London in the mid- and late 1960s. The small architectural practice in Bedford Square, near the British Museum, was called Fisk & Fisk, comprising Walter and his brother Sydney Fisk, an architectural technician called Gordon Dewar, myself and an office secretary. Two of the projects where I had some involvement were the overhead mail conveyor facility at Temple Meads Railway Station in Bristol, and the Post Office Telephone Exchange at Wakefield in West Yorkshire. In those days the Royal Institute of British Architects [RIBA] had a class of membership called Licentiate, for people who had worked as architects for years but had not qualified at a recognised college or university. Sydney was a Licentiate, whilst his younger brother Walter was a Fellow of the RIBA. And for a very few weeks before I began my architectural training, I worked for a firm called C. Frank Timothy Associates, a stone's throw from Fisk and Fisk, which had been commissioned by the then Ministry of Public Building ad Works to design a number of new prisons. One of the Associates [kind of junior Partners, but without the legal responsibilities of a Partner] was an architect called John Belcher, who was later completing his final design submission as a part-time landscape design student, at the same time as me.

6 MUM'S WORK FROM PRE-WAR TO WARTIME

So it was with little or no notice that my late mother Josephine Dita H. had chosen to follow me when I left home in the autumn of 1965 to study architecture. Dad had chosen to come and live at home, and mum knew that she wasn't going to be able to cope with it. She figured that if we went to London, I would be able to find an architecture course and she would be able to find a job as a secretary. She said she would be happy to work as a secretary in the Capital while I studied architecture full-time. Largely through a sense of responsibility for my mum's wellbeing, I went along with her plan.

In those days I was able to obtain a grant to cover both tuition fees and subsistence for an approved professional course at a UK university, even though it was means-tested. So it was a question of finding a course and finding somewhere to live. This was to prove to be a pivotal move for both my late mother and I, and indeed for my older brother John, since we were leaving him at home in East Suffolk, working as a jobbing gardener and managing the cottage on a day-to-day basis. The cottage we rented in Ufford had been our home for nearly twenty years thus far, and events would see us giving the home up for good.

For the last twenty or so years, I have been piecing together the jigsaw puzzle of my late mother's life prior to and during the Second World War, because she told my brother and myself next to nothing about this whilst she was alive. My late mother came to England in June, 1938, and her landlady/au-pair host was a Mrs. Brown [Braun?], of West

Acton in West London. I do recollect mum telling me that she worked in the former Osram light-bulb factory near Hammersmith Broadway and for Wolf Tools, also in London. The Osram incandescent lamp had been developed in 1906 and initially GEC imported Osram filaments from Germany for their own production of light-bulbs. By 1909, GEC had completed their factory in Hammersmith, and this became the Osram GEC Lamp Works in 1921. Wolf Tools was founded in 1900, opening their Pioneer Works in Hanger Lane, near Acton in 1935. They initially produced large cast woodworking power tools, producing their first DIY electric drill in 1949. The strategic importance of these two companies during the Second World War is self-evident.

My conjecture is that by the time that my brother John was born in September 1943, our late mother was living in or around Caversham, near Reading in Berkshire, and whilst my brother's birth-entry on the Register of Births, Marriages and Deaths did not state who his father was, it was replaced in 1944 to give my brother the name `Hutchinson' after my parents married in the Kensington Registrar's Office in Kensington in West London. Did mum and/or dad consider it to have been more publically acceptable at that time to be married now that mum was pushing baby John around in a pram?

John was born in the same temporary nursing home the day after Alison Filtness, the daughter of the late Donald and Nesbitt Filtness [née Murray]; Donald and Nesbitt were good friends of my late mother for many years after, even though the Filtness's lived in Lewisham in South East London, and we lived ninety-five or so miles away in Ufford, near Woodbridge. The Filtness's had married in the City of Westminster in late summer, 1942, and Alison's birth was followed by that of her brother Ian W M Filtness in the late summer of 1945, by which time the family had moved to Lewisham in South East London. I believe that Alison married a Wyatt in Lewisham in S.E. London] in 1965 and that Ian married a member of the

Spencer family in Bolton in 1967. When Donald died, his wife Nesbitt moved to near Dewsbury in West Yorkshire to be closer to Ian and his own family. She was to die there.

And we also know for definite that mum was a **stencil typist** at BBC Monitoring at Caversham Park near Reading in Berkshire between May 1944 [when my brother John was 8 months old] and February 28 1945, by which time she was only about 10 weeks off giving birth to me. I believe that typists at the time were given a waxed stencil sheet with a backing of substantial paper, bearing figures, scales etc. designed to assist the typist in cutting or preparation of the stencil sheet for duplication purposes.

The BBC in Caversham [still a listening station and now called `BBC Monitoring'] was not able to tell me much about her work as such, except this was at a time when all Monitoring's daily and weekly publications were indeed reproduced by the old stencil method. Mum must therefore have listened to the Nazi broadcasts and propaganda, and helped make that available to strategists guiding Britain's war-efforts. Mum was, for definite, living at Great Oaks, Goring Heath, when I was born in May, 1945, because that is what is says on my birth certificate. Furthermore, I've found an envelope from *Polyphoto*, this one based at Selfridges' Store in London's Oxford Street, and which contained tens of studio shots of dad and mum, probably just before the end of the War, [say 1944] and which was sent to mum, under the name `*Hutchinson*' at Great Oaks, Goring Heath in Oxfordshire.

The BBC Monitoring Service was set up in 1939 by the Government with the backing of the Pentagon to monitor the broadcasts of enemy countries during the Second World War. It provided information to both the BBC News division and the Government's Ministry of Information. It originated in a collection of wooden huts near Evesham, but moved in the spring of 1943 to its present home, Caversham Park, a 160-year old Italian baroque style stately home on the outskirts of Reading.

The nearby estate of Crowsley Park was acquired by the BBC at the same time, to act as the service's receiving station, and it is possible that our late mother was at the receiving station, because of her linguistic skills. Caversham Park and Crowsley Park continue to function in that role today. In a sense, it must have been paradoxical for her in the 1960s to know that the Soviet Union, once part of the Allied armies, was now part of the dangerous game of political chess being played out with nuclear pawns in Germany and beyond. Not that she would ever have remarked on the matter.

In another resurgence of the` celebrity/notoriety' theme, which, by sheer coincidence, crops up again and again in my story, Great Oaks, Goring Heath, had its share in the 1930s, when one of illustrious society-photographer Cecil Beaton's sisters, married a Sir Hugh Smiley of Great Oaks, Goring Heath, and at that time an officer with the Grenadier Guards. A chronicler of the Beaton family commented that Beaton's sister "had been spurned by Nancy Mitford. She wrote that she iiked his car and his income and thought him `awfully nice and kind in his own way……."

So how did it come about that mum was living at Great Oaks at this time? Well, Candida Lycett Green, the daughter of the former British Poet-laureate and renown architectural critic John Betjeman, gave me my first lead when she wrote on 18th February, 2011:

"There is no heart to the "village" of Goring Heath. It is a scattering of houses and cottages among a criss-crossing of tree shaded roads and lanes. It encompasses Cray ponds and Collins End and in the Second World War was alive with a busy RAF camp. The MOD requisitioned Great Oaks in its midst, a lavish Edwardian mansion set among rhododendrons with terraced gardens and views to the blue of fifty miles away. Temporary huts were erected of which odd vestiges and local memories still remain."

In military terms, South Oxfordshire already had a number of war time airfields due to the natural lay of the land, and the River Thames provided perfect training opportunities for the building of pontoons and Bailey bridges. At various times Americans, Canadians, Australians and Royal Engineers received periods of training on the Thames at Pangbourne. Howbery Park at Wallingford conducted similar exercises on the Thames for the Royal Engineers. Throughout the war years the propensity of empty stately homes locally provided ideal Headquarters for use by the Allied Armies. Two units of the 101st Airborne Division of the American Army completed their training for D-Day at Basildon Park, whilst the British Army used the Park for practising tank warfare. Coombe Park and Walliscote Manor House both in Whitchurch housed American soldiers and later ex Polish soldiers.

The Ministry of Aircraft Production [70MU] was based in part at Headquarters Site at Goring Oaks. The crates arriving there were believed to have contained aircraft spares, aero engines and sometimes whole aircraft, including Mustangs. Crates of English origin contained Spitfires. These aircraft were assembled at 70MU and loaded onto Queen Mary trailers. Mongewell Park Mansion housed the Royal Air Force from 1939 to 1945. In Goring, the Air Ministry trained Belgians who had escaped Nazi persecution to become pilots for the Belgian Air Force to fly in 349 and 350 Squadrons. The BBC moved to Caversham, forcing The Oratory School to re-locate to Woodcote, and both of them have remained 'in situ' ever since. Leslie C. Garton, of Garton Sugar/Tate & Lyle connections, owned Great Oaks House and Great Oaks woods and the surrounding land at the time, and was to accept the requisitioning of the property by the Government during wartime. The Oratory Preparatory School is now at Great Oaks, and I am indebted to Andrew Willson, Deputy Head of the Prep. School, for `filling me in' with important snippets of information about the use of Great Oaks during the Second

World War. Andrew told me that `the BBC requisitioned / bought Great Oaks for the duration of WW2 and used it essentially as a dormitory for a Y station - serving Station X at Bletchley Park.'* Does this mean that `Y station' was Monitoring at Caversham Park, serving the de-coding base at Bletchley Park? And that the listening-post at Caversham Park was part of a network including the King/Churchill/Heads of the Armed Forces? And was it the BBC that acquired Great Oaks, or was it the` MOD'? Anyhow, couldn't it be said that BBC Monitoring at Caversham Park was part of the War Ministry at that time?

I am also indebted to the BBC for providing the *Peoples' War* postings on the internet; these have enabled me to provide answers to so many questions that were bugging me about mum's life during the latter part of the Second World War. I have tried to select those excerpts from the BBC postings which seem best to describe the setting and context for mum's contribution to the war-effort, and have emboldened what seem to me to be most pertinent to my mum's situation at the time. The first description is by someone from Hungary [not so far from Vienna, geographically and historically!] who, like mum, came to work in Monitoring at the BBC in/near Caversham during the war:

*"Before the war I lived in Hungary. When the war was declared i was in San Merino. I came back to England to Sussex. In an [air-raid/bus?] shelter, **I saw an advertisement from the BBC for typists. I responded and was told to report to Wood Norton immediately and when I arrived and was allocated a billet I was told I would be on duty that night. I had to catch the BBC bus and started typing the daily digests and the Report of broadcasts all over the world. The Report was sent every morning to the King, Churchill and heads of the armed forces. I soon became a proof reader. This was very interesting because I knew what was going on. We worked on shifts throughout the day and night. We were not***

*always living in the best conditions. **Many of the monitoring team were foreigners** and this was very strange for the people of Evesham. The townspeople could not understand the needs of people working shifts even on Christmas Day, and would want to provide food or hoover when we wanted to sleep. We were called guinea pigs because the landladies were paid a guinea a week for having us. The whole department was moved to Caversham by special train. Because the work had to proceed without a break, we either worked a shift and caught the train with all our possessions or caught the train and worked our shift as soon as we arrived. **Some of us were billeted at Great Oaks.** Early in 1944, I had a major operation and spent some time in the BBC convalescent home. I returned to work in the summer until 1945, having heard the news of VE day leaning over the balcony of the reception hall. At the end of 1945, having married into the BBC, I moved back to Wood Norton."*

Denis Faulkner, a radio-engineer, provides my next excerpt from the aforementioned TV documentary series:

*"We had to live somewhere. **The BBC had earlier requisitioned a large two- storey country house called `Great Oaks' which was situated at a cross roads called `Cray's Pond'.** The road to the south led to Pangbourne, about two miles away. The road to the west led to Goring-on-Thames, also about two miles away. About a mile and a half north was the village of Woodcote. We understood that the house was the home of the chairman of a well-known sauce manufacturer who had had to leave it with all its furnishings etc. intact. **There were two driveways. The main one, from the Pangbourne Road, was not used other than as a footpath. The second was `the service drive' which came to the rear of the house from Cray's Pond. Here, there was a large stable block, which had been converted into dormitories, bathrooms etc.** All the males from Tatsfield,*

(apart from the EiC, SME's etc., …….. slept here. Each shift had its own area in order that there would be little or no disturbance to those sleeping during the day. For all other purposes we used the rear driveway to the house where we spent our off-duty time. **We ate in the dining room in `shifts' at different times to suit our working pattern.** *Interestingly, along one side of the dining room was a long table upon which dozens of small saucers were arranged. Each one contained one person's weekly butter ration and was labelled with each individual's name. Such was the trust we each had for each other, that no one had any fear of his ration being used by anyone else……* **Our `ladies' slept upstairs along with a large number of others who were employed at the Caversham Monitoring Station. These were nearly all typists and stenographers as well as secretaries. Many of these worked shifts too, in order to prepare the Monitoring Service Report, which was despatched to the government in London early each morning, by courier.** **At any one time there were not all that many people around, due to the shift system, there was however, a lot of 'coming and going'!**

With the help of my wife Lynne's distant cousin who lives in Caversham, Lynne and I have managed to locate the `nursing home' near Caversham where my brother John and Alison Filtness were born in September, 1943, and this is now a dormitory wing for an independent school called Highdown School, Emmer Green, and which is in Caversham Grove, Surley Row, Caversham, Reading. The 18th century building, altered and extended between 1878 and 1880 by a well-known architect of the period, Richard Norman Shaw, was thus to take on the Queen Anne style. His formidable design output numbers New Scotland Yard, on the Thames Embankment, London,(built as the headquarters of the Metropolitan Police between 1887 and 1906 and now known as the Norman Shaw Buildings); Cragside, a fine mansion in

Northumberland and Bedford Park, London, the first "garden city" suburban development: housing, including St. Michael and All Angels Church, 1879–82.

We also managed to locate the BBC's war-time monitoring station at Caversham Park, and, thanks to the kindness of the BBC's gate-keeper at the bottom of the drive, we were allowed to drive up to the house where my late mother worked, although we had to remain in our car at all times! Furthermore, given that mum was working at the BBC in Caversham from when my older brother John was 8 months old, and that our dad was serving in the wartime army at the time, where was John at the time? At this point in time, I can only conclude, by way of conjecture, that he must have been in a boarding-in nursery of some sort, and that this must have been the one that Jomo Kenyatta's son was also in at the time. Mum told me years later that my brother John [and possibly myself] attended a nursery alongside Peter Magana Kenyatta [b. Aug 11, 1943], the son by Edna Clarke, governess and English second wife [m.11.05. 1942, d.1995 aged 86] of Mzee Jomo Kenyatta, who was to become President of Kenya [64-78] after it became an independent nation within the British Commonwealth. Peter Magana Kenyetta became a Producer with the BBC in London before retiring. Jomo Kenyetta worked as an agricultural labourer in England as well as a teacher with the Workers Education Association to support himself during the War before abandoning his English wife in 1946 to return to Kenya and remarry. So Jomo Kenyatta was still in this country with his English wife in the spring of 1944, and Peter is only 5 or so weeks older than my brother.

The present building, inspired by Italian baroque palaces, was erected after a fire in 1850 by architect Horace Jones, who much later also designed London's Tower Bridge. During the First World War, part of the building was used as a convalescent home for wounded soldiers. In 1923, the Oratory School bought the house and about 120 hectares

(300 acres) of the estate's remaining 730 hectares (1,800 acres). The principal of the school was Edward Pereira. With the onset of the Second World War the British Ministry of Health requisitioned Caversham Park, and initially intended to convert it into a hospital. However, the BBC purchased the property with government Grant-in-Aid funds, and moved its Monitoring Service into the premises from Wood Norton Hall, , near_ Evesham in Worcestershire, in the spring of 1943. The nearby estate of Crowsley Park was acquired by the BBC at the same time, to act as the service's receiving station. Caversham Park and Crowsley Park continue to function in that role today.

Having left BBC Monitoring in March, 1945, when, as it happened, the end of the war was `on the cards', my mother travelled to Chippinghurst Manor in the Cotswold Hills in May, 1945, to give birth to me. Chippinghurst Manor, a very large manor house, set in parkland in rural Oxfordshire, dates back hundreds of years and has in the past been home to the nobility. More recently, it was the venue for a Football Association meeting to appoint Sven Goren Erikson as Manager of England's soccer team. Evidently, at least part of the building had been requisitioned during the Second World War to act as a nursing home for expectant mothers evacuated from London, which was being bombed incessantly. I have read that the Manor belonged to the McDougall family, famous for their flour, and they had given the Authorities use of it during the war. The Manor must have been the nearest nursing home in the Thames Valley area that was considered to be safe from German bombing, bearing in mind that Great Oaks at Goring Heath was still a risky location because it was surrounded by an RAF war-time training base that was relying on tree-cover to hide it from overhead enemy action.

I also know that my mother aspired to becoming a nursery school teacher at the time, and my unverified theory is that she had enrolled at the Rachel McMillan Teacher

Training College in Deptford, South London, which I think, ran a three-year full-time course for nursery school teachers leading to a Froebel Certificate in Education. Furthermore, given that the McMillan sisters Rachel and Margaret were early members of the Fabian Society and were Christian Socialists active in British politics and in campaigning for better education and health for poor children, and given that the Rachel McMillan College was at the forefront of nursery school teacher-training at the time, it wouldn't surprise me if the nursery school that my brother and Peter Kenyetta attended was the Peckham Open Air Nursery School run originally by Margaret McMillan, Rachel's sister. The BBC Monitoring Station at Caversham has confirmed to me that mum's address when she left their employ in March 1945 was 21 Gower Street, London WC1, which London University have confirmed was a property rented by them at the time and used as some kind of student centre [?hostel?]. The Georgian property has since been – and indeed continues to be - a hotel, and its layout would suggest that a hostel was a logical use for the building at the end of the war.

If my theory is correct, mum's introduction to education at the Rachel McMillan College had sown a seed of interest in the Montessori principles of education and she later told me how her interest extended to a `Free Thinking, Democratic' school called Summerhill, set up by AS Neill at Leiston in Suffolk, and which is still going strongly.

An early photograph of me as a 1+ year old kid in the garden at Ufford suggests that if mum did start on a nursery-training course in London, she could only have spent a short while there. Furthermore, I know that both John and I were sent to the private Deben Bank Nursery/Infant School in Woodbridge when I was 2-3 years old. I also believe that I was only 4 years old when I began at Ufford Primary School in our village.

The Deben Bank School seems to have disappeared virtually without trace, but I have traced an internet tribute to the life of a former pupil, an American woman who sadly died when she was young. She was called Tara Beth Brecher, came from Cave Creek, Illinois, and attended Deben Bank when she was a toddler in 1962, some 14 or so years after John and I were there. Her father served at the time at one of the United States Air force bases close to Woodbridge, which helps to explain his daughter's attendance at Deben Bank School.

7 EMBARKING UPON AN ARCHITECTURAL CAREER

I had studied architecture [mainly as a full-time student] - at what began as the Brixton School Building - for the requisite five years until 1971, excluding the year spent working for an architect [Fisk & Fisk] after the third year, and had then worked as an assistant architect for a number of architectural practices in London.

Brixton School of Building had been founded in the early 1900s during the heyday of *the Arts and Crafts* Movement. The college was incorporated into a converted building and housed both the crafts trades and a number of professional courses, notably surveying, structural engineering and architecture. However, at around the time that I enrolled at the college, fundamental changes were afoot in higher- and further education, foreshadowing the disintegration of colleges such as the one that I was joining. In its wisdom, the Government had chosen in the mid-1960s to concentrate all building-profession courses in universities and the newly-emerging polytechnics. One such polytechnic was the South Bank, incorporating the former City of Westminster College [with its business-studies focus] the National Heating and Ventilation College and the construction- professional courses of the Brixton School of Building.

It is amazing to look back at housing design during the time that I was a student: Our College was initially based in the London Borough of Lambeth before moving to new premises [now sold] in Wandsworth, and Lambeth Council was at the forefront of system-built high-rise, high-density housing schemes in the social housing sector. It was as if the pride surrounding the technical feat of pre-constructing these towers in temporary factories was at least as highly valued as the number of new housing units that were being produced. There were variants on this tower-block theme, notably the medium-rise, high density estates created by the neighbouring boroughs of Southwark and Wandsworth. Had the councils [and indeed Central Government] lost sight of the needs and feelings of the families being newly-housed amid the temptation of gaining political kudos through constructing these new large system-built schemes?

As we know, many of these new 'high-flying' social housing schemes of the 'Brave New World' are viewed very differently today, not only in London but across the country. Many of these estates have become slum districts where many residents fear for their safety because they have become centres for drug-pushers and other criminals; and a good many have now either been demolished or sold to private developers for modernisation as yuppie homes. You might say that, in hindsight, it was a major error to have ventured down this road.

So there we were, as students, studying the nitty gritty of concrete panel design, panel-joint technology, drainage systems, etc., demanded by high-rise dwellings, and Martin Wilkinson, our architect-lecturer in construction technology, was totally absorbed by the fascination of this new technology. We might have had sociology lectures at the time, but maybe the human consequences of the new dwellings that we were building had got lost in the process! The 1960s will mainly be remembered for the wrong reasons in British architectural history.

And, by way of contrast, architect Eric Lyons, president of the Royal Institute of British Architects, was beavering away in affluent Surrey, working alongside Span Homes in designing and constructing two-storey 'highish density executive homes' where landscaping played a more significant part in defining space and territory.

We students had to spend 6 months working in architects' offices at the end of the first year of the sandwich degree course that we had enrolled on, and I opted to work for the small country practice run by Roger Simmons and his fellow architect and business partner Philip Hunt. The office was on the village green at Claygate in the county of Surrey, and about 8 minutes' walk from Claygate station on the railway line from Waterloo to London Road, Guildford. The workload consisted of a mixture of bespoke houses for businessmen and housing schemes for local housing associations, along with car showrooms and other projects.

The printing technology in our rural office was a very basic dyeline machine, comprising a curved and illuminated glass exposure screen and a galvanised dustbin on a metal tray. A length of yellow coated light-sensitive paper would be cut off a roll and placed behind the tracing paper 'master negative,' the two being held in place by a relatively light-proof cloth which would be clamped down during exposure. The operator would then switch on the fluorescent light on the exposure screen for a fixed length of time and then take the exposed light-sensitive paper down to the dustbin, which was placed over some liquid ammonia on a tray. The ammonia fumes would then react with the unexposed part of the paper [i.e., corresponding to the lines of the drawing] and these would then change from yellow to blue/black. The resultant print would then be allowed to dry/air before being trimmed and folded ready to be posted.

Apart from drawing out new housing layouts, larger-scale plans, sections and elevations and detail-drawings, I was also involved in constructing housing scheme models, using coloured *Daler* board cut to follow the contours of the site, balsa wood houses and synthetic trees, shrubs and grass. And on occasions, I would accompany one of the partners or the senior assistant on site-surveys, using Dumpy levels, tapes and ranging poles. All this experience proved invaluable in later life.

The buildings were of modern cavity wall construction and with tiled roofs, and this was at the time when the architect Eric Lyons was involved in more 'modernistic' housing with more landscaping, working alongside Span Developments. Whilst we students were working in our respective architects' offices, the Royal Institute of British Architects' course-recognition group decided that our sandwich course did not meet their educational criteria, so, henceforth, we became full-time students.

Luckily, as a final-year architecture student, I had complete freedom as to what my final design scheme should be, as long as there was sufficient inherent complexity; and because I loved the countryside and everything to do with the Great Outdoors, I chose to design a national park study centre in Snowdonia. The challenges thrown up by this project included the fact that the site was a derelict farm on the hillside overlooking Maentwrog village, close to Tanybwlch and Portmadoc in the National Park; that the neighbouring buildings were constructed of local stone and slate; and that they were all of human scale, with the roofs often kept as low as possible through the use of dormer windows.

Mum's health made it difficult for me to focus as single-mindedly as I would have liked. Yet, thanks in great degree to the encouragement I received at the time from my design tutor Tony M, I persevered. I believe that in the end I had designed a scheme which truly solved the problems of marrying architecture with environment. The landscape was dominant and building was consciously subordinate, almost melting into the landscape.

The prime exponent of that principle in the *Modern Movement* in the architecture of the 1930s onwards was, arguably, the American Frank Lloyd Wright; he was one of my favourite architects, whose *Falling Water* house is a masterpiece in the Modernist vein. Nearer to home I admired the work of architect Ted Cullinan and notably his design for Minster Lovell Mill. This is a residential adult studies college in the Cotswold Hills, an Area of Outstanding Natural Beauty in the south Midlands in the UK. And, to my mind, the design reflects the humility of a designer called by the context, not-so-much to perpetuate, but rather innovate upon a local stone construction tradition expressed in the existing buildings that the architect incorporates into his new scheme. Builders have, historically, respected the craft-skills and logic of their predecessors in providing continuity in our human-scale environment. Had we any reason for changing this, even when we were innovative?

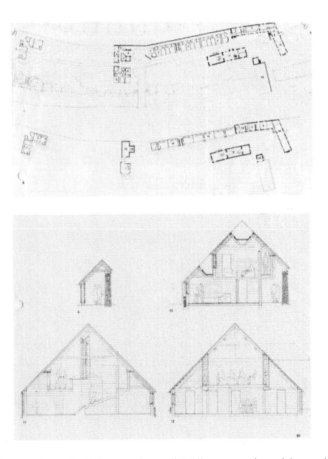

These plans for Minster Lovell Mill are attributable to the magazine *Architectural Design* of February, 1968

Imagine my delight at discovering that Cullinan's Uplands Conference Centre in the Hughenden Valley in the Chiltern Hills [another Area of Outstanding Natural Beauty, this time in Buckinghamshire], has been granted Listed Building Status. And I was doubly pleased to see that Georgina Livingston, a landscape architect who I remember as a very talented final-year student at Thames Polytechnic when I was later to enrol as a part-time landscape design student at that Polytechnic right at the end of the 1970s, was herself the landscape designer working alongside Cullinan on that Chilterns project.

8 PUTTING ARCHITECTURE TEMPORARILY ON THE BACK-BURNER

The 1970s wasn't exactly a boom period for the construction industry. I had now set forth on working in the real world in 1971. In the main, I enjoyed my architecture work, which had embraced acting as a project architect during the construction phase of a new indoor swimming pool at Crouch End in Haringey, North London, and working on the design of a new shopping centre in Camberley, Surrey, as well as on a Listed Building project [Floris the perfumiers] in Central London's Piccadilly. I was mentored in this latter fascinating task by a very experienced architect-colleague by the name of Keith Cotton, who was the salt of the earth to our firm and who would happily commute each day from Harpenden in the county of Hertfordshire. Keith was an accomplished violinist in his own right and loved to listen to Spanish classical guitar music played by Plácido Domingo.

In an amongst, so to speak, I had carried out some enjoyable detailing work on a new branch library in London's Southwark, across the River Thames from the Houses of Parliament, and on a new speculative office block in the City of London. The new, single-storey brick-walled library was the subject of a planning gain contribution by the developer arising from planning permission for a commodities exchange building in Southwark. The London Borough of Southwark had therefore invited our firm to implement the library rather than giving the scheme to it's in- house architects or other consultants. By now I'd moved from Leonard Vincent's office in Portland Place – and between Broadcasting House and

Regents' Park - to Ronald Fielding's office in the Aldwych, Holborn. My desk overlooked Bush House, then the hub of the BBC's World/European Service; at the time I did not appreciate the significance of the European Service to my late mother's early years in London.

The years 1974 and 1975 were a difficult time for the nation's economy, and the larger commercial architectural practices such as that of my new employer were increasingly seeking work in the Middle East as a means of survival. On reflection, it seems extraordinarily indulgent that our developer-clients should be `shelling out' a fortune on cladding very high, glistening, steel framed speculative office buildings in the City, clothed at street-level in thin slabs of mottled blue/grey marble and dark-coloured anodised aluminium glazing systems. But I concede that, unlike Chester or Bath, the City of London did not have a distinctive vernacular heritage to build upon! And it is even more incredulous to (metaphorically) watch from the side-lines today as many of these commercial buildings have already been bulldozed to make way for even taller office- and apartment towers.

When I was asked whether I would contemplate a move to the UAE/Dubai, I declined, and eventually chose instead to work for a small firm of architects which had, years earlier, overseen the restoration of a number of Christopher Wren's bombed churches in London, as well as the design of the [old] *Financial Times* building in the City. My employer was now the firm Richardson Houfe, whose client-base had changed dramatically by the time that I joined them, although its architectural reputation lingered on.

Professor Sir Albert Richardson of London University established the practice with his son-in-law Eric Houfe, and the professor's last masterpiece, undertaken in collaboration with his son-in-law, was Bracken House in the City of London for the *Financial Times*, designed in 1954. By this time, the once-progressive Edwardian was perceived as a conservative reactionary......but the Professor had the last laugh, albeit posthumously, for Bracken House became the first post-war building in England to be listed.

Our workload now included bespoke, classically-designed new homes for businessmen as well as the adaptation of a cottage in Buckinghamshire for the actress Hayley Mills. She and her first husband Roy Boulting purchased Cobstone Mill and Cottage in 1971, and extensive conversions and remodelling of the interiors were completed as well as interior and exterior restoration and conversion of the mill. I believe that the property was sold a few years later, when Hayley and Roy separated, and it seems that it was at this point in her life that Hayley asked our firm to adapt a brick-and-knapped flint cottage that she had now bought for herself. I would normally be the first person in the office in London's Wimpole Street because I was still living in the West End, and it would not be too long before the phone rang and I would be trying to answer Hayley's new queries on the kitchen she wanted, or whatever else to do with her new home that she was anxious to sort out. Then there were the telephone calls from the Administrative Manager of much-visited Waddesdon Manor, the former Baron Rothschild mansion in Buckinghamshire now owned by the National Trust. My boss was the consultant architect to the Waddesdon Manor Estate, and our office secretary delighted in answering these calls, practicing her well-rehearsed posh affectation.

And, surprise, surprise, when I was later to work for Clifton Nurseries, we bought plants by the lorry-load on a regular basis from the nursery at Waddesdon Manor.

One of my projects at Richardson Houfe was a company director's new house in the Kentish Weald. This is a tract of land lying between the chalky North- and South Downs in the county of Kent and comprising rocks of the Cretaceous- and Tertiary age that are exposed at the surface as a thick sequence of sands, clays and limestones gently folded into an upfold [anticline] known as the Weald Dome.

Workwise, it was for me a completely different kettle of fish and taught me early on that as many rules and regulations were flouted as adhered to, and that the protection of professional indemnity insurance policies called for prudence in these instances.

More to the point, having steered the project as far as the placing of contracts, we resigned as architects and left it to our erstwhile client to appoint the builder and see this 'mischievous' project through to completion. Briefly, the client, a north London steel stockist, had purchased a planning permission for a single storey agricultural worker's dwelling, having supposedly been misled by his solicitor as to the nature of the permission. So, having had successive applications for larger [two storey] dwellings on the said site turned on by the County Council, the client [from the other side of 'The Pond'] proceeded to commission a large, elaborate, classically-symmetrical 'dormer' bungalow, **without** the dormers but with the first-floor lit by Velux lights ultimately inserted on the rear-elevation by the client. The 'legitimate' windows and doors were capped by 'flat' brick arches constructed from purpose-made soft- brick 'rubbers' or voussoirs, which were skew-shaped bricks slightly wider at the top than at the bottom to prevent them dropping under load from the wall above. I had to draw each arch to full-size for the purpose of manufacturing these brick 'specials', and in doing so, I had to build-in a subtle rise in the centre of the underside of the arch to overcome the visual illusion that the arch was falling! I think the technical term is '*trompe l'oeil*'! The brick manufacturer then produced these 'specials' – at no little expense - either by cutting the brick in its green state before firing, or by using a specially shaped mould.

By this time I had developed itchy feet, and, being single and without child-dependents, entertained the idea of widening my professional expertise by becoming a landscape architect. I had gained my Diploma in Architecture and could have settled at proceeding to sit my Professional Practice exams as an architect. I'd enjoyed the work that I had undertaken to a degree, although it wasn't particularly challenging. Working [at Ronald Fielding] on new speculative offices on the site of the old *Daily Telegraph* building in London's Fleet Street didn't do anything for me, and commercial architecture was, I felt, too narrowing, too egotistical, didn't provide any real public gain and failed to encompass contextual design. Furthermore, through my late mother's contacts at the Architectural Association's School of Architecture in London's West End, I had the good fortune to 'have an audience with' architects such as Sir Peter Shepheard, who themselves had progressed to becoming landscape architects as well.

Was this cheekiness on my part? Yes! After all, I was just a country bumpkin trying to 'come good' in London! Sir Peter was a Visiting Tutor at the School of Architecture, and his own architectural practice [Shepheard, Epstein and Hunter] was handling projects such as the master-planning of the new city of Salford – adjoining the city of Manchester - and the new University of Lancaster. And Sir Peter was later to become Visiting Dean of Architecture at Penn State University in the United States. And I was doubly fortunate in having the design offices of Sir Geoffrey Jellicoe and Howard V. Lobb a few doors up from my digs as well as that of Sir Frederick Gibberd a mere four minutes' walk away in Percy Street. As an architect, landscape architect, town-planner and garden designer, Jellicoe (8 October 1900 – 17 July 1996) was to win great acclaim for his landscape design work at Sutton Place near Guildford for J. Paul Getty and his JFK memorial at Runnymede. And Jellicoe had close ties with Thames Polytechnic [Greenwich University] where I was a part-time landscape design student. Furthermore, Sir Frederick was able to introduce me to Dame Sylvia Crowe, who master-planned the landscape for Gibberd's New Town of Harlow and the drowned-valley reservoir known as Rutland Water in Rutland / Leicestershire.

In my own small way, I was enthused by the prospect of having dual design qualifications; and was driven partly by disenchantment of career-advancement opportunities in the London area during a significant slump in construction , with the inevitable consequences for construction of another bout of `boom and bust' spells for the nation's economy. With my eyes fully open, I therefore embarked on what was to become a career in landscape design. I had chosen to make a complete break with architecture and treat a job in landscape gardening as a truly `hands-on` grounding for a professional career that would also embrace landscape design.

So I made the break in early 1975. Henceforth, on my many trips to customers over the next four or so years, I graduated from being the innocent country bumpkin into having, let's say, a smattering of awareness of the `multi-faceted life' of the Capital. I worked at grass- roots level [literally and metaphorically!] as an operative for a much smaller landscaping company in Pimlico, close to the Royal Hospital, home of the renowned Chelsea Flower Show.

The `bread and butter' work for the small landscaping firm that I joined in Pimlico, near Victoria Coach Station, included gardens-maintenance, new planting and landscape construction on a small scale. What was pleasing was that we operatives worked as semi-autonomous pairs, meaning that, apart from some special days, we were able to organise our own daily timetable. There were the richer customers such as film-director John Schlesinger [with his extensive roof-garden], who allowed us to decide on the extent of summer bedding, as well as the routine periodic maintenance calls — with tea and biscuits thrown in - at the home of actress Billie Whitelaw [Mrs. Robert Müller]; the luxurious Edwardian house in Chelsea rented by Roman Polanski, the Rolling Stones and Donald Sutherland; the modernistic town-house of film-director John Schlesinger; the Georgian Kings Road,

Chelsea pad of Lady Lambton [County Durham aristocratic roots]; and the Thames Embankment studio home of cartoonist Gerald Scarfe. Our visit to that studio, ostensibly to carry out some garden maintenance in the courtyard beyond the studio, was a real privilege and a joy to behold, with huge cartoon roughs hung from all the walls of the room making the experience somewhat surreal. We couldn't but stand in awe at the artist's ability to make every deft stroke of his pencil, pen, and charcoal and paint- brush so telling.

And by way of contrast, we enjoyed our regular unofficial exercise in below-budget landscape enhancement for a housing association in Poplar, part of London's East End, where plants and bricks that had been cast off by our wealthier customers, were more than gratefully received and put to good use. If the weather turned inclement, we could always stop by at a good old taxi-drivers' café not so far from the Chelsea football ground until the heavy rain had passed over, this being the café which, I believe, the losing side on Lord [Alan] Sugar's *Apprentice* BBC TV programme would 'retire to' before being brought back into Lord Sugar's boardroom to face up to the possibility of being 'fired!' And if we were experiencing a prolonged period of drought-conditions, as in 1976, then we simply had to postpone grass-cutting and focus our energies of helping the more vulnerable trees and shrubs to survive. I well remember etching out a shallow groove around the circle of roots of a Birch tree in a private West London square, in order to pour in washing-up water supplied by the square's gardens-secretary, so that the tree's roots might reach some scarce source of water. And there was the roof-garden that we had to construct for the female boss of an 'upmarket' brothel off Notting Hill Gate in West London. This was indeed a 'seedy neck of the woods', and, during that period, I came to be ribbed more than once about my naïve ignorance of cosmopolitan 'life'!

This period was transitional for me in more senses than one. In relation to living accommodation, mum and I had to make some key decisions. Reluctantly, we had to give up our bed-sit rented accommodation in the West End and so rented a first-floor flat in Statham Grove, Stoke Newington in North London, very close to Clissold Park and five minutes' walk from the Highbury Stadium, which at the time was the home ground for Arsenal Football Club. What was of sole significance for us at the time was that the flat that was in a smallish late Victorian terraced house that had recently been acquired on a buy-to-let basis by Christopher C., a City stockbroker and Anne F., his property-investment partner. It was 1977 and there was limited availability of private-sector rented housing stock. To put this into its historical context, the 1918 figures that showed the private rented sector to be around 76%, with home ownership at just 23% and public housing at just 1% homeownership. Now fast-forward to the late 1980's when private rented accommodation slid down to about 8-9%, after which it started to grow again. Home ownership stood at about 70% in 2003.

We were one of three groups of tenants in the house, and the rent we paid was a hefty one, even in London terms. Increasing rent-levels had signalled a spurt in the entry of new private landlords into the marketplace, so it was not surprising that, after about a year, and with the arrival of a Labour Government in Westminster, the Rent Act was soon enacted and put into operation. One of the components of this legislation was Rent Control, whose aim was self-explanatory, and we three groups of tenants chose to challenge the rent which we were paying through the newly-established Rent Tribunal system. Our tenancies became regulated by the Act and were henceforth known as 'protected tenancies'. What the Act did was to change the underlying law for the tenancies it applied to, in three main ways:

It introduced rent regulation;

It introduced long term security of tenure; and

It introduced new rules of 'succession' which change what happens to the tenancy after the tenant dies.

The Rent Act was exceedingly unpopular with landlords. Indeed, it has been described by one disgruntled landlord as 'expropriation without compensation". I really can sympathize with the `sound' landlords who come across rogue-tenants unprepared at the outset to ever pay any rent, but the real world isn't always an honest one. Unsurprisingly, the combination of being liable for repairs —whether or not they ever carried them out — and being unable to charge a `proper' rent or `easily' evict tenants, resulted in many landlords selling up and investing their money elsewhere.

The legislation was, therefore, anathema to our landlords C. and F., who at the outset had naturally sought to maximise their return on this property investment. None of us tenants was therefore surprised when we received eviction notices from the local court fairly soon after we had been awarded Fair Rents. In `legal-speak', the reasons why a landlord can evict are set out in Schedule 15 of the Act and consist of some 20 'cases'. These are divided into 'discretionary' and 'mandatory' cases. Thus, possession under the discretionary cases will only be granted if the Judge considers it reasonable to do so. Under the Act, all protected tenants have a right to apply for a 'fair rent' to be registered. Once this is done, this rent is the ONLY rent which can be charged. The landlord can apply to have it reviewed every two years, but not otherwise, unless there is major improvement work carried out to the property or some other substantial change to the letting. As time went by, the rents assessed by the Rent Officers, which were supposed to relate to the 'market rent' drifted down and down, mainly because there were very few proper 'market rents' to compare them with.

The year was 1977, and, the grounds for eviction were limited and specific for tenants such as ourselves who ensured we paid our rents on time. Ingenuity was evidently required! Ms. F. therefore postulated that now she required the entire house because, she evidently claimed, she was now expectant. I could not attend the hearing as one of the tenants because I was at work, but I remember clearly being told by one of the other tenants that Ms. F. had arrived in court with a concealed inverted pudding bowl next to her abdomen. The judge accepted Ms. F.'s grounds for re-possession of the property and we were all 'given marching orders' soon afterwards. I have been reliably informed that whilst records of the official registration of a fair rent on the property can no longer be traced by civil servants, this does not mean to say that they do not exist! But I have traced a record of Mr C. living in London N1 in 2001, and I distinctly recall reading about how whole squares of Victorian houses in the London N1 area had been totally rebuilt from within, during the previous two or so decades. Not that were was necessarily any connection!

Nowadays we are hearing calls for the re-introduction of rent-controls in response to claims that tenants [especially those in London] are being exploited, and are finding it increasingly difficult to remain close to their families and friends. The retort is any such legislation would be flawed like that in the 1970s. Further it is argued that we as a country should be building more homes to satisfy demand, though it seems that there is a low take-up for the government-supported scheme to encourage first-time buyers to buy new properties with the help of a moderate deposit. Such is the price of new properties that it is increasingly difficult to raise any kind of affordable mortgage on them. The depletion of the social housing stock is due not simply to sitting- tenants exercising their 'right to buy' option, but to local authorities [as social landlords] standing by whilst their estates become so run-down that they cannot afford to rectify them. Local authorities, notably in London, are subsequently selling them for the land they sit on – notably to overseas investors - to raise the finance, it is said, to repair the balance of their housing stock.

And the new, replacement high-density tower blocks of flats are being let at very high rents to the likes of yuppies, with only a small percentage allocated to the affordable rent sector and the affordable [shared] ownership sector. Predictably, a 'them and us' scenario develops and fish and chip shops and Turkish takeaways are no longer welcome components of the mix. Coincidentally, just such a case is Woodberry Down, on the short bus route along Green Lanes from Statham Grove to the nearest tube station of Manor House. It is just one recent example of where the local authority — seen in the fading past as the steward of the community's housing stock heirloom — has arguably failed in its task, insofar as there has been a significant reduction in the net social housing stock due to this development, and a weakening of the cohesiveness of the local community. In their article in *The Guardian* newspaper on 18th May, 1914, writers Aditya Chakraabortty and Sophie Robinson-Tillett suggested that what we were seeing here was the 'gentrification' of the estate. They noted how one former tenant had exercised her right to buy [a lease in this case] before being told that the whole Woodberry Down estate was going to be sold for redevelopment over a period of years, leaving her with no option other than to sell the lease to the local authority and move 80 miles out to Ipswich in Suffolk to buy an affordable home. She now has to make monthly journeys into London to meet up with her grown-up children and friends.

Furthermore, given the size of land banks held by builders and developers and the effect of this on land prices, the cost of new homes has led many potential new buyers to look instead to the private rented sector in the interim. And even when planning legislation [i.e., Section 106 Agreements] has attempted to create a percentage of affordable housing in new housing schemes, builders have understandably sought to avoid this commitment by, for example, breaking up developments into unit totals small enough to allow them to fight shy of providing affordable new housing. One such advert on the internet goes as follows:

Affordable Housing and Section 106 payments aren't always inevitable, we can advise on how to avoid or significantly reduce them.

If the profit margin for your scheme is pushed to below 17.5% by Affordable Housing or other Section 106 payments, we can help. The demands made by local planning authorities should not jeopardise the viability of any underlying planning permission. In these cases we can prepare a Viability Assessment based on properly documented building costs and sales values, helping you to negotiate a significant reduction in your Affordable Housing provision or Section 106 payments.

The bottom line was that we three tenant groups in Statham Grove [including ourselves and the McPhersons] found ourselves homeless, and that, because I was a single male adult with no children, I was not eligible to be given priority on the housing waiting- list for our local authority, the London Borough of Hackney. Not only that, but my earnings were subject to a particularly hefty deduction by way of income tax precisely because I was a single person without child-dependents.

Historically, the concept of renting a home from a 'public' body in the UK is quite new. The cottage we grew up in was built by the Lord of the Manor for his workforce in the 17th century and we had other 'tied' cottages/houses in our lane, as well Almshouses to house the needy. And some of my friends lived in cottages tied to local farms, etc. It was only through the circumstances resulting from the shortage of homes for discharged servicemen after the Second World War that the lord of the manor in Ufford was compelled by new legislation to make the cottage available to families unconnected with his estate but seeking accommodation in the district. Council housing built by local district councils to be let to families putting their name down on a waiting list is quite a new concept which was rolled out on a far bigger scale in cosmopolitan London, Birmingham, Manchester, etc. than in what were small, isolated rural communities such as Ufford. The Woodberry Down Estate in north London is a case in point, and we have seen peaks and troughs in the construction of rentable social housing from the early 20th century onwards, reflecting the political priorities of successive governments. As things stand, citizens cannot rent such social housing as of right, and, indeed, demand far outstrips supply. Furthermore, as we have seen with Woodberry Down, whilst social rents might be significantly less than in the private-sector, it is surely not accidental that there is no local public audit body/agency which would require local authorities as landlords to maintain their properties in good condition. The likely cost to the Exchequer would rank with the likes of our National Health Service! Given that most of the funding of local authority services is now dependent upon annual government grants that are by far the biggest part of their income, and given these have been drastically cut as I write, local communities have become decreasingly democratic by the mathematical inverse square. Just one of the many knock-on effects is the under-investment has increasingly led to a large proportion of these properties becoming very sub- standard if not uninhabitable. Demolition then becomes inevitable and a significant proportion of the electorate has lost out. But at what cost in the broader sense and in the longer run?

Families must fend for themselves in an increasingly hostile housing environment, especially in the private-sector rental arena, and the availability or otherwise of money to put down as a deposit on a property is crucial to their setting foot on the first rung of the property ladder. There may be no available council/housing association properties for grown-up children of social-housing tenants, but there will be social mobility for the determined folk who, given the opportunity, are prepared to fight their corner, irrespective of disadvantage or disability. Many such folk move on in life from being children of working class households to becoming skilled tradesmen, businessmen and professionals and, often, property owners or renters in the private sector. In other [European] countries, including former Communist-states, home-ownership may be the exception rather than the rule, so, to that extent we might be seen by some 'outsiders' as being somewhat indulgent in the UK! Anyhow, I acknowledge that I am revisiting the notion of the *Nanny State*, but recognise that there are dangers in being overly-dependent on the state, especially in relation to being able to openly criticise our 'over-lords' who we might be dependent upon for the roof over our heads or for our livelihood. In short, we are talking about a degree of control over people's lives which does not necessarily marry well with the healthy exercise of human rights. Equally, an over-dependence on private rented-sector housing, arising from a combination of unaffordable house-purchasing and the unavailability of rentable social housing, again leaves people particularly vulnerable, especially to exploitation. As I write, we are encouragingly beginning to see a widening of the scope of procurement, using various 'self-build' models involving the release of land by land-owners that include local authorities, which latter may often hold the biggest stock of land in any particular area within the UK.

Increasing urbanisation of our regions has put enormous pressure on the countryside and its smaller villages, with the consequence that property prices there have escalated unimaginably. It is therefore likely that many new rural households will be unable to afford to set up home near their parents, leading to a radical socio-economic restructuring of the community. 'Gentrification' is an emotive term that was used in the *Guardian* article in relation to the Woodberry Down estate in North London, but, nevertheless, describes a very real and significant process that needs discussing in relation to the socio-economic changes that have taken place in Ufford since I left there.

Clearly, since by now, neither my mother nor I contemplated returning `home' to our cottage in Ufford, our only sensible option at this point in time was for me to purchase a flat in or near London at a price which allowed me to take out an affordable mortgage. So both of us began to search for a flat, and in the interim we resigned ourselves to staying at a small hotel/guesthouse in Islington, though we were glad to leave at the earliest opportunity! One of the `joys' of our short stay there was the false-alarm fire alarm that woke us all up in the middle of the night, whence we had to make our way along a musty-smelling basement- corridor to the escape door, lit only by the emergency lighting. Thankfully, we were able to find a small flat in Shepherds Bush which was one of 50 flats in a 1950s block of flats, and I was able to take out a mortgage on the property in 1978. The [mis-]management of this block of flats is, though, another story that I will relate later.

9 SAILING CLOSE TO THE WIND, WITH CLOSE SHAVES AND NAGGING QUESTIONS TO BOOT

In 1979, a job advertisement appeared in the *Gardeners' Chronicle and Horticultural Trade Journal* [G&HTJ] for a Landscape Designer and Contracts Manager at Clifton Nurseries in Little Venice, close to the Regent's Canal, Maida Vale and Edgeware Road. To cut a long story short, I applied for the post and got it, and whilst, for the most part, I enjoyed working there, and my job was secure enough, it was not going to be a `job for life'. It was nevertheless an excellent platform for me to train to become a practical landscape architect, and for that I shall always be grateful.

Our nursery-base was only a stone's throw from St John's Wood and a bit further from Abbey Road, then Swiss Cottage, Hampstead and Finchley. All this meant that we were in a prosperous part of the Capital and with a customer-base that included a good number of Jewish families. The Hamlyn's, of publishing fame, were one such family, and Mrs. Hamlyn was frequently on the phone to our Managing Director to organise garden-maintenance and new seasonal planting. Jane Asher's late mother was another such customer, though she was not `high-profile' in the sense that the work our firm carried out for her near the `immortalized' Abbey Road in London's St John's Wood was small-scale `one-off' landscape construction-work. Besides which, Mrs. Asher was a quiet, charming and quite unassuming person, with no `airs and graces'!

So what was the link between helping rebuild Jerusalem in the later twentieth century and building big new greenhouses in the proximity of London's Maida Vale and Paddington Railway Station? Answer: Jacob Rothschild. And where did I find `philanthropy' in leafy Hampstead? Answer: the household of the Lebanese millionaire Albert Abela.

I believe that Clifton Nurseries [CN] was established in the early twentieth century by a Mr Cohen -a typically Jewish name if ever there was one – though, even if I ignore business-acumen, I doubt that he was somehow an ancestor to the Cohens who were the founders of the Tesco supermarket chain! When I first joined the firm early in 1979, the Chairman of the Company was the elderly Lord Drogheda, who would infrequently call in at the offices. On Lord Drogheda's death it was to be sold to the merchant- banking arm of the Rothschild family, partly, I suspect, because Jacob Rothschild owned property virtually adjoining our premises. I will nevertheless concede that, as one of the wealthier people in Britain and with a well-known ancestral pedigree in horticulture, he might just have been driven by financial- and horticultural-motives as well!

It so happened that around this time, and with Bob the lorry driver leaving after notching up a good many years' service, our landscape division was to find itself temporarily without a lorry driver whilst the replacement post-holder was `detained at a certain person's leisure'. And so, pending the engagement of a `temp' lorry driver, my Landscape Director boss and I took it in turns in driving the lorry to deliver building materials when we could not get them to be delivered to our construction-sites by the suppliers. So, during the school summer holidays, daughter Beth Rothschild volunteered to help us with these deliveries, which she enjoyed. Sitting high up in the passenger seat of a lorry-cab was a novelty for her and gave her a scenic view of passing streets and pedestrians.

The next three-to-four years were to be a roller-coaster ride in the fast-lane for me as I combined working `all hours that God gave me' with part-time study to train as a landscape architect. Finished was the hands-on garden maintenance work, the construction of timber fences, the summer bedding-plant schemes for the wealthy clientèle and the odd tree-surgery task. Gone too were the PJs [private jobs] which my erstwhile colleague Andrew W. and I had undertaken for cash on light summer's evenings or on Sundays. My old boss had not minded us using the firm's van and all the tools that it carried, so long as the PJs were outside business hours, but this was now consigned to past memories! As too were the memories of travelling as a passenger along London's Kensington High Street, behind a stream of traffic, and suddenly discovering that the foot-brake of the vehicle you are travelling in fails to work as you draw nearer and nearer the car in front and need to brake sharply……. Hand-brakes and first-gears did have their uses, after all! And so did old-fashioned hand-signals when I occasionally drove around Hyde Park Corner in the firm's old `army-style' Land Rover with the right-hand indicator deciding not to cooperate with the vehicle-driver. And in those days there were no traffic lights on this famous London roundabout! Needless to say, we drivers – including myself on L plates - had to remind our boss on numerous occasions that not only were our lives at stake, bit our driving licences as well!

At CN, my typical new working day started at 7.45am, by which time I had taken a bath, shaved, grabbed a bite of breakfast at home and driven eastwards down a relatively empty Westway [the urban motorway from the White City to Marylebone, via Paddington] before the rush-hour had begun in earnest.

Gaining my driving licence had opened the way for me to change jobs and to enjoy the benefits of a company car. And this more or less coincided with my enrolling on a part-time landscape design course which had begun life in West London but which was to move out to Wilmington near Dartford in Kent on the creation of Thames Polytechnic. I had 'graduated' to having a company car – a 1.3 litre Ford Escort hatchback -with petrol provided - which was indeed a valuable perk; and, luckily, this was before the Government began taxing these perks as earned income. From my employer's perspective, I had become responsible from the inception of landscape design schemes to their completion and invoicing, and I had to ensure that an acceptable profit margin was achieved. From my own perspective, I would never have been able to have undertaken the landscape design course without the free use of the car, which not only allowed me to travel to and from a campus that involved a good hour's travel across the Thames, around the South Circular and out into North Kent, but also the ability to reach the locations in North Kent chosen by the college tutors as the sites of major design projects. Then there were the journeys to horticultural gems such as Hidcote Manor Gardens in Oxfordshire and Westonbirt Arboretum near Bristol and Swindon, all easily achievable in a day's driving there and back.

However, over a period of time it became clear that the company-car 'perk' was begrudgingly given in certain quarters of the firm's higher echelons, such that on one occasion when I was due to take my 'day release', I was informed that I would not be granted the use of 'my' company car.

A well-known truism goes something like: *"To them that hath, more shall be given. And to them that hath nowt? Who cares?"* I could have resorted to self-pity when informed about my use of **my** company car, but I resolved not to. For, even though I was given little warning, the amount of time I did have, allowed me to call in at the Abelas' household to undertake a bit of pre-planning...... The Abelas were on our maintenance rota when I was with my previous firm, so that I was already on good speaking terms with the chauffer, who knew that my present employer now had the lucrative maintenance contract for the extensive garden. The significance of this was that the individual, who had withdrawn my use of the company car on the day I was off work, might just have valued the Abelas' custom....... Mr Abela's company was, after all, one of the wealthiest in the City of London, not to say globally.

The result of my initial move was that the chauffer gained Mr Abela's agreement to my borrowing the `household' Ford Capri, which car the chauffer normally used for general `running around' when he wasn't driving either of Mr Abela's two Rolls Royces. I therefore caught the tube-train from work to the Abelas on the night before college and was given the keys to the Capri, a car a good deal more powerful than mine, **and** which the chauffeur had already filled up with petrol. I duly returned the car and the keys early in the morning after college, with the tank duly topped up from my own pocket. The routine was repeated for at least two weeks after this, by which time my employers' `upper echelons' had got word of events. The upshot was that, from thereon in, I was granted the use of `**my'** company car on my college-days, though I guess that this must have rankled somewhat, especially since a work-colleague, based in the houseplants division, wanted to have day-release to study but was denied it.

There was the odd occasion when I agreed to let my colleague have the use of the car over the weekend, in which case I would borrow one of the vans if it was available. On one occasion there was neither car nor van to drive, and, since I needed to take some site photographs for one of my student projects, I borrowed the lorry. On the following Monday morning, the lorry driver showed his head around the corner of my office, and enquired as to why the tachograph on the lorry was showing a steady 50 mph for a period of half an hour or more the previous Saturday. The answer was simple: I had been travelling down the A2 in Kent and there wasn't too much traffic on the road! The driver shook his head, smiled wryly and shuffled out of the office, cynically tut tutting all the way..... And, anyhow, we looked after each other in the landscape division, and I had been one of a small group to insist at the outset upon the lorry-driver's reinstatement once he had served his time of 'detention at H.M's pleasure'. This was despite the fact that the company chairman [Mr. Rothschild's predecessor] and two of the three directors - but not my immediate line-manager/Director - were eager to sack the driver in his absence. The 'dismiss-him' group's strange logic implied that the driver had somehow brought shame upon the company, when there was no such connection to be made, because the said offence took place before the driver joined our firm, and the person concerned was truly repentant for his actions.

On occasion, our firm would tender for landscape work designed by architects or landscape architects, and this gave us a refreshing change from pricing our own designs. I was privileged insofar as one of the firms that would submit tender enquiries was the late Preben [Ben] Jakobsen's design-office. Jakobsen was a highly respected Danish landscape architect and garden designer with a distinctive clean formality / modern classicism about his work; and his schemes would include business park landscapes and office roof gardens in London and elsewhere, as well as gardens for 'discerning' individuals. I guess that he was confident that, if we were awarded the work, we could faithfully translate his designs, which was a compliment in itself! And I loved working in horticulture as a landscape designer and contracts manager, especially since I was working with plants of every description and designing not only in three dimensions but also with time as the fourth dimension. The love of horticulture and working with nature knows no class-boundaries, embracing society as a whole, from young people to the elderly.

Needless to say, in my student-*persona*, I thoroughly scrutinized all Jakobsen's immaculate drawings to glean all the knowledge I could! After all, he also happened to be one of my college's external examiners, though it was not appropriate to talk about business matters when, at college, he was providing me with a testing critique on the work I was submitting. Robert Holden was another landscape architect who would seek quotations from our firm for his design work, and he was also visiting lecturer at the time I was a part-time student at Thames Polytechnic [now Greenwich University], as was Derek Lovejoy. Robert was later to co- deliver the professional practice evening lectures which I later travelled down to London to attend when I was working in Leicester and just prior to qualifying professionally; he subsequently took over Headship of Greenwich Uni's Landscape Design Department.

One of the enduring memories of my spell of employment at CN was of the office secretary continually reminding the Financial Director that the business practice of unduly delaying the payment of suppliers was unfair. The second is on a work-culture that demanded that employees devote their whole energies to their employers for well in excess of the contractual hours, without being remunerated for the said `overtime'. Failure to do so was viewed as an expression of disloyalty, and I had to constantly remind myself at the time that, in this respect, my loyalty was with me and my late mother as much as with my employer. We both had lives to live beyond my working hours. My late mother was, after all, expecting me home at a civilised hour in the evening, so that we could share supper together before we were too tired to enjoy the meal that she had shopped for and prepared. I was working slightly in excess of the required 40 hours a week, even if it was over 4 rather than 5 days, and this was no different to the `flexi-time' that was being introduced at around this period by progressive employers who really respected and valued their staff. And I made sure that my work did not suffer because of it!

When asked eventually – and no prizes for guessing who posed the ultimatum - whether I wanted to be a landscape architect or remain as landscape designer/contracts manager, I chose the former, since I was nearing the end of my landscape design course and was not going to sacrifice all the time and energy I had committed to the course thus far. Given that I was temporarily jobless, money was now extremely tight in the hectic run-up to submission of my final design scheme, and I regularly woke up at around 4 o'clock in the morning and retired late at night, just to produce the drawings before my deadlines. I shall never forget the night that I had to return back home to central London from a long day and evening at college in Dartford, and had no return ticket. It was around 10 pm that the suburban train pulled into Dartford, destination London, Charing Cross, and as luck would have it, the carriages were the type without a corridor, meaning that there wouldn't be an inspector on the train. So, having negotiated the busy ticket barrier at the Charing Cross main-line terminal at the end of that stage of my journey home, I only needed to buy a single underground ticket from Charing Cross Tube Station to reach home, which I accepted submissively. When I arrived home at getting on for midnight, I had to admit to myself that the journey had been a little hair-raising!

My interest in landscape restoration had been kick-started by this final college design scheme, and I was subsequently to be commissioned by the earlier-mentioned *GC & HTJ* weekly magazine to write a series of articles on this topic, taking me [by train of course, and on day-return fares!] to Stoke upon Trent, Liverpool, Gateshead, the Rother Valley in South Yorkshire and the china clay tips of Cornwall. These assignments helped me survive until I found my first job as a [virtually] qualified landscape architect; and they were great eye-openers, especially in relation to the true extent of toxically-contaminated urban waste-land that represented a less palatable – yet possibly unavoidable - aspect of our Victorian industrial heritage.

10 REFLECTIONS

Mum had gained 'naturalised' status, and thus gaining UK citizenship, when we were young – if not before - and, significantly, and had opted not to seek joint Austrian-UK citizenship either for herself or for us boys. As a young boy, I did not understand the significance of this and was not really concerned. We were British citizens with British passports, and that was all there was to it. I vaguely remember seeing mum's original Austrian passport, with one of its bottom corners cut off, and, I believe, with a Swiss border-control stamp in it.   However, I had never thought it strange that neither she nor we as a family had ever gone to Austria. Mum had a small photo-album which she kept locked up in a brown leather suitcase under her bed at home in Ufford, and I do recall the time when my dad had allegedly broken into it when we were away. Mum didn't trust dad, and this mistrust had, I guess, contributed in part to my dad working away from home for nine or so years. Even when he came home for the odd weekend break, he slept on the bed-settee in the living room (not that mum had told us anything much about the birds and the bees, as children!) Did dad leave of his own volition or under duress? I may never know.

As for the relationship between my mum and my brother, this is something that I will probably never fully understand either. John was a supportive son in our youth, and Mum was not generally expressive of her inner thoughts and feelings. I do remember once instance when my brother had saved up to buy a bass-drum, and I'm not sure whether she had been fore-warned or was entirely happy about it. Anyway, the low-pitched resonance of this instrument is hard to escape from, especially in the confines of our tiny cottage, and can therefore be irksome as an unwanted noise-source.

If drum-noise at home was ever an issue between my brother and my dad, when mum and I left home in 1965, this was for them to sort out! Given that I had the requisite `A' level passes to be awarded a student-grant, and given that London seemed the best place for me to study and for mum to find work, that's where we headed in the summer of that year. Dad's arrival back home was imminent, and mum could not countenance staying at home in the circumstances.

However, security of tenure of the cottage was in the forefront of my mum's mind, and I well remember the Saturday mid-morning meetings mum had with her trusted solicitor in Woodbridge, a partner in the firm Gross and Curjel, to ensure that the tenancy was still in her name and not dad's. This way, she reckoned, she could be sure that John had a roof over his head and we had a home to fall back on, whatever my dad chose to do.

John has said next to nothing to me about how he coped living at home with our dad. My dad had to give up his job as a labourer on the Sizewell `A' nuclear power station, when he was involved in a site-accident. A deep trench had been excavated, but its sides had been inadequately shored-up. As a consequence, several men, my dad included, were injured when the sides caved in. It was disappointing to hear from my dad that, despite prolonged delays in arriving at a settlement, the trades-union that he and his injured colleagues had belonged to did not achieve a fair amount of compensation for the men. My father was off work for several months, but to his great credit, he had hitherto never failed to support mum financially when he was at work, and had sent money to her in London every week by registered post. He could no longer do that, so, as a student on a means-related grant, I thankfully had my grant re-assessed.

When dad was eventually able to return to work, he found a job in the storeroom of the large, early 1900s building housing Woolworths shop in Woodbridge, and then as a gardener at Dougy Goldsmith's Crown Nursery in upper Ufford. I believe that he remained there until his retirement. Not that I am certain, because, by 1970/71, John had decided to 'up-sticks' and move to London. My brother did not have a job in mind or anywhere to move to, but, for whatever reason, he was struggling to cope with remaining at home with dad, and any fear of the unknown was outweighed by this pre-occupation.

Mum had certainly given John a good grounding in coping strategies when we were growing up; she had encouraged us both to take part in a one-month long Outward Bound course at Holne Park, Ashburton, on the edge of Dartmoor, in the summer of 1962, and we had subsequently persuaded the local education authority sufficiently of the merits of this endurance-testing course to be awarded a grant to cover the cost of the course fees and the travel to Devon and back. A lot of the participants on the orienteering-type course were sponsored by their employers, including a number from the RAF, etc. I recall how we had to jump from the wall of a stone bridge into the fast-flowing river at the entrance to Holne Park - every morning that we were not trekking across Dartmoor or Exmoor - and how one of us held the hand of a colleague as he finally plucked up courage to take the leap after steadfastly being too scared to contemplate the jump. Nights spent sleeping under bivouac sheets tied to massive stone boulders on the isolated moors, miles from civilization, with no money to speak of and only a compass, a map and some Parkin cake rations can never be forgotten!

During the first three or four years of our being in London, mum and I had travelled home to Suffolk every weekend, to be with John and make sure that the cottage was OK. I had a large drawing board in our bedroom in the cottage, and used to get on with design projects over the weekend, often working late into the night with the help of my angle poise lamp clamped to the drawing board, with an

124

extension lead stretching over the upper landing, down the stairs and into the living room below, where I connected it to the bayonet light fitting. We only had a socket outlet in the kitchen, which was used for the Wee Baby Belling and the electric kettle. I won't say that the power supply was the safest, but, given our shortage of money, we as tenants could not afford to have the cottage properly wired up.

Amongst the design projects we were set at college were a new kibbutz in Israel and a nursery school in London. I cannot recall mum saying a great deal to me about *kibbutzim*, but she was particularly interested in the school project, because nursery schools were `after her heart!' She dug out a couple of text books about nursery education which she had hung onto since the end of the war, and these helped me understand the principles behind nursery education. At a philosophical level, both projects could be said to have had a `socialistic' thread running through them, and that was `par for the course' at the college at that point in time.

Our Saturday morning routine was to get the early train from London Liverpool Street to Ipswich, then catch the local train to Woodbridge. Our first port of call would be the Dairy Tea Rooms in Cumberland Street, where we would have a milky coffee. We would collect any post from the main post office next door – where mum had arranged for own post to be re-directed - buy the weekend shopping at the local shops, then catch the bus to Ufford, generally from Melton Hill. We would then prepare Saturday lunch and chat and read the local *Woodbridge Reporter* weekly newspaper which we would have bought in Woodbridge. There were generally things to be done in the garden and around the house, and, when these were added to time needed for my student design-projects, my weekend was fully accounted for.

11 GOODBYES TO HOME UFFORD

Mum became seriously ill around the time that John left Ufford, meaning that our weekly trips home to Ufford came to an abrupt halt. Hitherto, very early on Monday mornings, mum and I had taken a pre-ordered taxi from home to the railway station in Woodbridge, to catch the early train to Ipswich and then on to London Liverpool Street Station. So sudden was mum's setback that we could not warn the taxi driver, besides which, we were not on the phone in Ufford. This occasion was to mark the beginning of the cessation of our ties to home and my dad. From then on, our cramped rented accommodation near Bedford Square in Central London was to suffice as our `official' home as far as we were concerned.

John was soon to leave dad alone in Ufford and find himself London digs and employment. His short stint as a kitchen hand and then as a barman in the plush staff-restaurant of Lloyds Underwriters in the City of London was followed by two spells at Selfridges, first on the bar in the store's public restaurant, then as a salesman on the sales-floor of the large department store. Happily, mum and I were eventually able to meet up with John when mum had recovered, and the three of us would occasionally go on Sunday bus rides to places like Kew Gardens or Syon House.

Despite choosing to keep a certain distance from my brother – she had her unsaid reasons - Mum was always at hand to encourage him and advise him when he felt unsettled and was contemplating changing job. Whilst this contact diminished as the years went by, John was to form his own circle of friends, and mum and I pursued our own lives.

Dad meanwhile, had been left to cope the best he could, and, by the mid-late 1970s, had relinquished the cottage in Church Lane, Ufford to Gordon Easton, who had been landlord and owner of the property for nearly ten years. Dad was in his early 60s by now, and was contemplating retirement. Mr Easton had not undertaken any improvements to speak of when dad was there on his own, and a move to a warmer, drier and more modern home was therefore long overdue for him. And he would have a bath/shower and W.C. at last! In around 1981, mum and I decided that we would drive up to Suffolk in my company car to visit dad, and, not finding him in Ufford any longer, we made some local enquiries, and managed to track him down to his rented housing association bungalow in Churchman Close, Hall Farm Road, in the neighbouring village of Melton.

I think mum wanted only to be sure that dad was OK and happy, and he was. The small bungalow was ideal for him, and he didn't have the worries of the old cottage in Ufford. I guess the owner of the cottage saw it differently, because he was now able to sell the property in Ufford in a period when the social make-up of the village was changing rapidly. Thus, whereas the Agents for the Blois Brooke Estate had offered in 1965 to sell the cottage to us, as sitting-tenants, for £1000, by the time that dad moved out, which was in the mid- 1970s, its value as a vacant freehold property in the extended London commuter belt must have been a great deal more. The property was on the market again around 2008/10, and the next-door half of the cottage (now known as 3 Lady Cottages in Church Lane, Ufford,) was sold in 2011 for just under £250,000.

It was in the 1960s that an architect/town-planner called Graeme Shankland was commissioned to prepare a plan for the expansion of the town of Ipswich, eleven miles from Ufford. Peterborough was another town earmarked for orderly expansion at the time. Ipswich, as with Peterborough, was no longer simply an important market town in a predominantly agricultural region of Britain. Its relative proximity to London and its burgeoning population made it the target for significant urban expansion, with the knock-on effects on employment patterns and house-prices that this implied.

Should I therefore be surprised to see that one property newly constructed on land at Ufford Place (this had been the land comprising the manor house and its formal gardens occupied by Colonel Blois Brooke when I was a child), was sold for £250,00 in November 2005, and then for £546,600 in June 2007?

And, to underline the staggering changes to the village, we now have Ufford Park Hotel, Golf and Spa near where the former World War two Nissan huts had stood and had accommodated families after the war. Significantly, one of today's Sunday broadsheet newspapers ran a feature article on the extent of property price increases in `desirable' locations, noting that prices had tripled over a short period of time, with the consequence that local families were being priced out of the property market. What we are witnessing is a widening social revolution that has accompanied a fundamental change in the country's economy, the rapid mechanization of agriculture, the decline in heavy industry and the greater importance of the services sector to the economy.

12 UFFORD, VIENNA AND PAN-EUROPEAN UNEASE

The 1960s had seen the heightening of East-West tension that we know as the Cold War, and, as kids, our direct experience of its outward appearance was the constant drone of fighter-aircraft over our cottage in Ufford. Periodically, a much larger USAF transporter aircraft flew very low over our home, and its noise was deafening. We had two military bases near Ufford, fairly close to each other: USAF Bentwaters and RAF Woodbridge, which was actually in Sutton.

To a degree, USAF Bentwaters was self-sufficient, but a number of the American personnel lived off-camp in neighbouring villages, including Ufford. One of these was the Herndon family: Reb and Ruby, together with children Chris and Maureen. Mum had got to know Mrs. Herndon, who, with her family, lived in an old timber-framed house on Upper Street, at its junction with School Lane. I guess that mum and Ruby had a great deal in common: Ruby was a Londoner by birth, and mum had lived in London for a number of years. Both had two children of similar age, although mum was a bit older than Ruby. Reb was, I believe, a fighter pilot, and had elected to serve two tours of duty in this country. Ruby was [and still is!] a gifted abstract painter. Furthermore, both Ruby and mum liked to read the *National Geographic* magazine, with its topical articles on the world-scene, its fascinating articles about journeys of discovery and its excellent photographs. We had first come across the *National Geographic* magazine when another American family that had been renting a cottage in Spring Lane, lower Ufford, wanted to clear out their possessions before leaving. We were therefore delighted when Mrs. Herndon passed on her copies to us.

Mum did well to make ends meet with the limited income from her wages and dad's. However, this did not create any barrier whatsoever to friendship between the Herndon family and ours. I recollect that long after the Herndons left to return to the USA, they sent us gift-subscriptions for the *National Geographic* every Christmas.

I was delighted to speak to Ruby again a number of years ago. She and her late husband Reb, who married in Bedford in 1943, returned to England on husband Reb's retirement from the USAF, and settled in North Cornwall, where she was able to develop her career as an abstract landscape painter. A Londoner by birth, Ruby had studied painting on the occasions that she had travelled back to the States with Reb's reposting. Sadly, Reb died a while back. Their son Chris was born in Derbyshire near the end of World War Two, and younger sister Maureen was, I believe, born in the States. Whilst both Chris and Maureen are now living in the States, Ruby has flourished as a painter in Pelynt in Cornwall, expressing on canvas her stated aim of abstracting the spirit of the Southwest landscape on to a two dimensional surface.

Though they never discussed it at home, mum and dad must have been acutely aware of the background to the Second World War and the Cold War, in their different ways: dad had served in the British Army in the Second World War, and was conscious that the Soviet Union's army eventually formed part of the Allied Forces' pincer-action that eventually cornered Hitler's army on the European mainland. As discussed earlier, Mum had been part of the BBC's listening/monitoring team based at Caversham Park, near Reading. She had therefore listened-in to Nazi German broadcasts day-in and day-out, including propaganda directed towards Europe, and had helped make this material available as part of Britain's war-time effort. Having no doubt kept tracks of the USSR's rôle in Austria's murky post-war` re-constitution', it must have been concerning for mum that the Soviet Union, once part of the Allied forces, was itself to become the aggressive player confronting the US, Britain and other [western] countries in a Cold War that was being rolled out across Europe and beyond. And this was within two years of the declaration of the end of the Second World War.

Karl-Heinz Vögler, our German scout pen friend of our teens, faithfully kept in touch, and I remember the postcard he sent us from Berlin, which showed President Kennedy outside the Brandenburg Gate, then part of the notorious Berlin Wall. All I knew was that Berlin had been divided after the Second World War, along with the rest of Germany, and that the eastern part of the city formed a part of the huge Eastern Bloc that was the Soviet Union.

I distinctly remember how, on the news bulletins on the BBC's Home Service, we were to learn of the grim fate of desperate [East] German freedom-seekers as, by night, they tried to cross the river separating the two halves of Berlin, or tried to crawl under the barbed-wire fences keeping the Berliners apart. The beam of a *Stasi* searchlight would pick out their silhouette in the darkness and then a bullet-sound would ring out to break the uneasy silence as yet another brave attempt at escaping from the clutches of the East German border-guards ended in failure. The East German régime, calling itself the GDR/DDR [*German Democratic Republic*], was a *Stasi*-led police-state puppet-administration under the jurisdiction of the Soviet Union, supported at `grass-roots' level by those East Germans who spied on their neighbours with the aim of trapping and betraying any dissident voices. Years later, attempts were made to destroy the paper-trail of evidence that would expose the guilty, but this material is today being pieced together to act as a record in perpetuity of the actions of the *Stasi* and its `grass-roots collaborators in post-war Eastern Germany.

The Soviets, as one of the *Occupying Powers* following the cessation of the Second World War, had `inherited' part of the erstwhile capital of Germany as well as the eastern half of Germany as a whole. The Soviet Union had subsequently constructed the Berlin Wall to divide Berlin, the main aim being to prevent the younger and gifted citizens of the eastern side escaping to the West. Such a brain-drain, on a significant scale, would mean that the fragile economy would fail and lead to the downfall of the GDR. I clearly recall how talented [East] German athletes would travel overseas as team-members, seemingly to represent the GDR at sporting contests, only to slip the net of team-security on arrival, disappear, only to re-emerge at the government offices of host-nations, seeking political asylum. I can only surmise at what mum made of all this, because in general, she scarcely vented her feelings on these issues. What was different, seen from the perspective of a family living in Britain, was this: that her perspective was that of an [erstwhile] Austrian citizen who knew deep-down that a sense of normality had not returned to her home country, and that, for the foreseeable future, at least, it was unlikely to.

The destinies of Germany and Austria were to follow different paths in 1945, but the two countries had certain things in common: Austria, like Germany, was divided into four occupation zones and jointly occupied by the United States, Soviet Union, United Kingdom and France. Vienna, like Berlin, was similarly subdivided but the central district was administered jointly by the Allied Control Council. Whereas Germany was divided into East and West Germany in 1949, Austria remained under joint occupation until 1955; its status became a controversial subject in the Cold War until the warming of relations known as the Khrushchev Thaw. After Austrian promises of perpetual neutrality, Austria was accorded `full independence' on 12 May 1955 and the last Occupation troops left on 25 October that year. However, it would be a serious mistake to believe that the period between 1945 and 1955 was uneventful for Austria, let alone Germany, Russia and the whole of the remainder of Europe.

Yet British school-children are at risk even today of gaining an overly 'Brit-centric' view of events before, during and after the Second World War, and therefore never come to fully appreciate the complexity of events across Europe [and indeed the Near East] during that decade. 'Repatriation' took on a new meaning during that period, when the repercussions of war-time allegiance to Nazi Germany included death-sentences for hundreds, if not thousands of Cossacks, ethnic Russians and Ukrainians who had been forcibly 'returned' to the Soviet Union by the British Government, amongst others, to suffer their fate. The repatriations were agreed to in the Yalta Conference attended by Churchill as Britain's representative; most of the 'repatriated' people were Soviet citizens, although some of them had left Russia before or soon after the end of the Russian Civil War, or had been born abroad. Those Cossacks and Russians were described as fascists who had fought the Allies in service to the Axis Powers, yet the repatriations included non-combatant civilians as well.

Mum had been born in Vienna in Austria, shortly after the end of the First World War and the beginning of a redrawn Europe. Prior to that war, Franz Ferdinand, born near the end of 1863, had been an Archduke of Austria-Este within the Austro-Hungarian Empire, and Royal Prince of Hungary and of Bohemia. From 1896 until his death, he was heir-presumptive to the Austro-Hungarian throne. His assassination in Sarajevo in late June, 1914, along with that of his wife, precipitated Austria-Hungary's declaration of war against Serbia. This caused the Central Powers on the one hand, including Germany and Austria-Hungary, and the countries allied with Serbia or Serbia's allies on the other, to declare war on each other, starting World War 1. Franz Ferdinand and his wife had been guests of the British Royal Family not so long before their murders. Then there was the rôle of the Soviet Union in the Second World War, which mum must surely have followed closely whilst working at BBC Caversham.

As I write, events have been taking place in Belgium and this country to mark the one hundred years since the beginning of the First World War. The TV cameras have honed-in on German- and British graves side-by-side in a Belgian war graves cemetery, whilst the current President of Germany, and royalty and political leaders from both Britain and Belgium have been to the fore, reflecting the shared sense of loss by Britain and Belgium on the one hand, and Germany on the other. The two sides had fought each other so bitterly, and with such a tragic loss of human life. Yet little has been said in the reporting of these commemorative events about the factors giving rise to the so called `Great War', and the rôles of other states in the conflict. Were these rôles significant in the pan-European and pan-global picture? Certainly, mum never discussed the First World War with us as kids, never mind anything to do with Austria. Seen in retrospect, mum's silence on the matter was understandable, given that we were British kids, and that she wanted to foster our sense of British identity.

My knowledge of Austria was abysmally scant, and we learnt next to nothing about recent political history when I was at school. Instead, history lessons had focused introspectively on the Industrial- and the Agrarian-Revolutions in this country, as well as royal successions. Furthermore, in the run-up to my GCEs, a last-minute switch by our history-teacher at Ipswich Civic College meant that our class had been entered for O-level political history, which was our replacement history teacher's specialism, even though we had learnt about British economic history up until then. As a class, we were thus ill-prepared for the questions on the British Monarchy and the English Civil War which confronted us. Events in Europe in the later nineteenth- and early twentieth centuries were therefore an area of our understanding which we had by-passed. And more recent events in what had been

British Colonial Africa meant nothing to me as a teenager. The *Kikuyu* uprising and the *Mau-Mau* insurgency in Kenya, and its link with Jomo Kenyetta, were miles away from childhood-life in Ufford.

13 STARK TRUTHS

When mum wanted to help me with research for my architectural history assignment in the later sixties, I did not understand the deeper significance of the architectural history specialist she had innocently but well-meaningly approached. The topic of my essay was *Palladian Architecture*, and one of the recognised British authorities on the subject was **Sir Anthony Blunt**, then the Professor of Architectural History at the Courtald Institute in the University of London. Mum was working as a secretary in the University's Institute of Education, which was based then in one wing of the Senate House, the huge 1930s Portland Stone monolithic headquarters of the University, at the back of the British Museum in central London. Whilst mum was aware of Sir Anthony's position in the University, she did not know at the time that he was also the Queen's advisor on art-history. I do not recollect meeting the man, but he gave my mother some useful leads to pass on, in terms of background-reading.

We were therefore totally amazed when, some years later, Sir Anthony was apprehended as a key-figure in Soviet espionage in the UK. True, a near-neighbour of ours in Ufford had once volunteered to mum that, whilst he was employed by the RAF as part of the team monitoring the East Coast of Britain at the height of the Cold War, he was also a member of the Communist Party. But Anthony Blunt's arrest was of a different order, as was his subsequent suicide. I knew nothing about any of the constituent republics of the Soviet Union, only that the Ural mountain range divided European Russia from its Asian counterpart. Nor did I know anything about the specific rôle of the Soviet Union during and after the Second

World War, especially in Austria and further east, never mind the activities of the *Gulag* and the fact that Nikita Kruschev was in charge of the Soviet Socialist Republic of the Ukraine before becoming President of the USSR. Whilst I was unaware at the time of my Ukrainian connection, I was well aware of the stand-off between the West and the Soviet Union during the Cold War, the dangers posed to East Germans, not to mention `Russian' Jews, seeking to escape to the West or Israel. I knew that Nikita Kruschev and Bulgarin presided in turn over the USSR after Stalin, and it was they who were the counterparts of John Kennedy and other US Presidents of the era. I was also aware that Soviet dissidents were being sent to Siberia for daring to criticize or challenge the Soviet régime and that a number of top athletes from the Soviet Bloc took the opportunity to seek political asylum in the likes of the USA when they travelled to the West as part of their national teams.

Mum had told me that she had taken shelter in Underground Stations when Hitler's bombs fell on London, and dad had spent every day in the army not knowing where he was going to be posted and whether he would survive from one day to the next amidst the bombing and fighting going on around him. So, not having been told anything about war-time experiences by my parents, could I put myself in their positions?

It is only in later years that I have come closer to truly appreciating the danger confronting both my parents during the war. London was the subject of a huge and prolonged bombing effort on the part of the Germans during the war, and the destruction and loss of life was huge. And, in response, the Brits were determined to wrap the whole war up in 1945 with a bombing raid to end all bombing raids, Hiroshima apart. And In a television programme marking the 70th anniversary of the Allied bombing of the German city of Dresden, viewers came face to face with the grim reality of all-out destruction as a result of relentless British bombing, fire-bombing and of an unimaginable inferno in which some 250,000 Germans died. Such was the ferocity and intensity of the bombing and so intense were the fires that raged across the city that people not killed directly by the bombs, were sucked into the heat and unable to escape alive. Victor Gregg, a surviving British prisoner-of-war imprisoned in Dresden at the time, was a witness to events, and whilst he did not blame the British pilots for dropping the bombs and fire-bombs, he still cannot forgive Churchill and his wartime cabinet for the utter scale and inhumanity of the attack. He said that it took him 40 years to come to terms with what he witnessed in Dresden, so how long did it take mum and dad to come to terms with what they experienced during the war, if ever? .....

Thanks to being shown a letter that dad had written to his sister Alice in North Shields, Tyneside, just before he and his fellow soldiers embarked on the highly risky crossing to Dunkirk as part of the Normandy landings, I am came to appreciate his feelings at that moment in the war. Dad implied in his letter that it really was going to be a matter of life or death for him and his fellow soldiers in the coming hours and days. Dad knew well that every word he wrote in the letter was being censored before it was sent by military post, but he was not unduly worried about that because there was nothing in the truth that he was expressing which could have been seen as being `sensitive'.

Being tea-totallers, mum and I did not frequent any pubs during the whole time that we lived together in London, nor did we belong to any leisure-activity groups, except that I had joined the London Central YMCA club as a student, and enjoyed learning more there about photography. We both enrolled for French-speaking and conversation classes at the *Institut français* in Kensington, West London, which we thoroughly enjoyed, and mum would occasionally visit the German cultural institute when she had time on her hands. Mum also took a keen interest in the architecture of the 1930s, and, because we lived so close the Heals' furniture shop in Tottenham Court Road, mum took it upon herself to approach Ambrose Heal with the idea that there should be a 1930s Society in the same way that there was a Victorian Society. **The 1930s Society** was later to be launched, and this later changed its name to The present **Twentieth Century Society** (sometimes abbreviated simply as C20) which campaigns for the preservation of architectural heritage from 1914 onwards The Society was formed as *The Thirties Society* in 1979, the year in which the Thirties exhibition was shown at the Hayward Gallery on London's South Bank. The society's interests extend to buildings or artefacts, whether important or humble, rare or commonplace, that characterizes twentieth-century Britain. Though several modern buildings had been listed on the recommendation of Nikolaus Pevsner in 1970, it was felt that much more needed to be done.

Sir Nikolaus Pevsner, a Jewish wartime refugee and an architectural historian famous for his authoritative Penguin Books' *The Buildings of England* series, had his small office near the College of Preceptors and overlooking Bloomsbury Square. This was Virginia Wolf territory, including Drury Lane, Russell Square and the British Museum / British Library. The new British Library on the Euston Road was still on the drawing board at the time. I would regularly see the bespectacled Sir Nikolaus hard at work in his front office when I passed by on my way home from college in the 1960s.

I was not 'into politics' in any active way when I was studying for my A levels in Ipswich, and whilst I would occasionally buy [the then 'centrist'] *Manchester Guardian* national daily on my way to college, I cannot say that I was attracted by the idea of joining some fellow students on weekend Campaign For Nuclear Disarmament [CND] marches to Aldermaston in Berkshire.

I had been introduced to Virginia Woolf, the Fabians. Sydney and Beatrice Webb, and the roots of the British Labour Movement when I was studying modern English literature at A level. And later, as architecture students, we had looked in more detail at the life and beliefs of William Morris, artist, designer and Socialist. And many British Socialists were proud of the work and thinking of these pioneers, identifying themselves with the founders and leaders of the Soviet Union. Yet, for mum's part, Communist-subversion in the workplace was one of her `bêtes-noires'. She had come face-to-face with subversion earlier in life, when working in Woodbridge, and was to witness it again later when working in the head-office of a large Anglo-Dutch company based in London. The Anthony Blunt revelations were to come not so long after.

Simply seeing where the Webbs were `coming from' is one thing; the broader reality of life in the Soviet Union, especially for <u>Soviet dissidents</u>, following the deposing of the Tsar, was, arguably, another.

Put very simplistically, Hitler had, on the one hand, chosen to **eradicate European Jewry** by setting in place a huge-scale meticulously planned `ethnic cleansing' operation. He saw these Jews as a major threat to his Great Dream of creating a much-enlarged *Germanic* state peopled by pure fair-haired and blue-eyed Germanic compatriots.

On the other hand, the leaders of the Soviet Union had chosen to **rid/cleanse the USSR of its `bourgeois'** by herding them and sending them to what was effectively long-term / life-imprisonment in labour camps, or *Gulash*, distributed across the USSR, where they would be forced to undertake forced labour **in conditions that would eventually kill millions of them.** And they were indeed shot `point-blank' in their hundreds and thousands – and oft-times on an arbitrary basis - if they refused to work or slowed down, even through sheer illness or exhaustion. The Soviet *Kremlin / Politburo's* argument was that the tables needed to be turned on the privileged, moneyed-classes of the Tsarist era who they claimed as having traditionally exploited the proletariat through low wages and dreadful living conditions. But that is not to say that life was much easier for the `labouring-classes' of the Soviet Union, especially when you place the establishment of the *Gulash* in its historical context. Witness the breakdown of the Nazi-Soviet pact, the invasion of the USSR by the Nazis early on in the Second World War; the enormous loss of life suffered by the Russians as they bid a hasty retreat in the face of the Nazi onslaught and joined the Allied Forces in opposing Hitler's forces; and the innate poverty of the Soviet Union throughout the whole of the WW2 and well beyond.

In 1970s London, our main love at weekends and during holidays from work had been to travel and to visit towns, parks and gardens of interest. Before I passed my driving test, we made best use of bus-travel concessions available to us in London, notably the one which allowed us to travel as far as any single bus went on Sundays. Thus, we would frequently take the 73 bus from Gower Street, in London's West End, all the way to its destination in Richmond in Surrey. We would then spend the day walking along the Thames riverside or visit Ham House or Richmond Park – with its deer -before wending our way home at tea-time. We also enjoyed strolling to the launderette in Georgian Lambs Conduit Street, near to Charles Dickens' ` home-territory' in Doughty Street, Lincoln's Inn Fields. Our route took in Russell Square, the Italian Hospital in Queen's Square, the National Homeopathic Hospital and the Great Ormond Street Children's' Hospital; and it was the Italian Hospital that mum later chose to go to in the first instance, when, around 1969, she fell seriously ill with Phlebitis, the inflammation of the wall of a vein, even though the private hospital was not part of the NHS. Happily, mum's GP at the time was a doctor at both the Italian Hospital and the large NHS Whittington Hospital in Highgate in North London, and he was able to oversee her seamless transfer to the larger hospital when she was well on the road to recovery. We would also take the same route to reach the newish Theobalds Road public library, which was a joy to use, with such a good stock of books and a public meeting room. And in the summer we loved to sip tea outside the coffee shop in Russell Square, with the sound of the nearby modernistic water fountain partially drowning the drone of the traffic on the surrounding streets.

Mum enrolled as a part-time HND Business Studies student at the City of Westminster College in the late 1960s, and by this time the College was a constituent of the same South Bank University that I attended. She found this course especially stimulating; particularly in view of the years she had hitherto spent working in business in one capacity or the other. One of the major projects which she had opted to undertake as part of the course was a study of the creation of the new Rhine-Main-Donau [Danube] canal, the construction of which was drawing to a close at the time. This canal now allowed ships to travel up the Rhine from Rotterdam and the North Sea, make their way along the River Main and then proceed downstream along the River Danube, all the way past Austria towards the Black Sea. I was working in an architect's office at the time, doing my `year-out' stint, and I took some days' holiday so that I could accompany my mum on a journey along part of the route of the canal. We took the ferry from Harwich-Parkeston Quay to Bremerhaven, then a train via Hamburg to Nuremburg, which lies on the canal. I had not studied political history at O level or A level, and so did not know at the time about how badly Nuremburg had been bombed during the war, and how it had been the venue for the post-war trial of leading Nazi figures who had been particularly instrumental in the deaths of millions of European Jews.

14 THE FATE OF MUM'S FAMILY: ADDING 2+2

So I think it is appropriate at this stage in the book to look closer at the events which eventually led to the Nuremburg Trials. In particular, what was I to conclude, after mum had died, if I was not conscious that she might just have had any relatives in Austria? Simply that either mum had no wish to contact them or that there were none to be contacted? Why indeed did Mum never show any [outward] inclination to even visit Austria ever again from the time she set foot in England to the day she died? This was my starting point when I took my first tentative steps to test the validity of my suspicions via the internet in 2001. At that time, there was just my wife Lynne, our adoptive son Daniel and myself living at home in West Yorkshire, and we had only been on the internet for a very short period of time, perhaps two years. In those early days of mass-consumer internet-use, we were dependent on a connection via a second telephone line, and, since this was quite expensive, we had to be frugal in the use of on-line time.

As a family, in my childhood and youth, we were not outwardly politically minded, though mum must have been aware of the situation in her homeland without saying as much to any of us. It would probably be over- simplistic to say that, having worked on the 'home- front line' in BBC Monitoring during World War Two, she will have kept a passive eye on what was going on in Austria immediately after the war, when the states that were now 'calling the tune' [i.e. Britain, the Soviet Union and the US] wanted to portray a notion that Austria was now a neutral state, because, in reality, things were not so clear-cut in Austria at the time. The Allied occupation of Austria lasted from 1945 to 1955. Austria had been regarded by Nazi Germany and countries as far afield as in South America, as a constituent part of the German state, but in 1943 **the Allied powers agreed in the** ***Declaration of Moscow*** **that it would be regarded as the first victim of Nazi aggression, and treated as a liberated and independent country after the war**. Were the Western Powers in denial? And were non-Jewish Austrians also in denial? After all, the ***Anschluss*** had taken place precisely because of the willingness of Hitler's native Austrian sympathisers / collaborators from the later 1930s onwards – if not before that decade - to aid and abet the *Führer* in an organized and pre-meditated manner. So how, in retrospect, could Austria have been perceived as an **occupied nation** during the war in the same sense as, for example, Belgium, the Netherlands or Norway? This really did seem to stretch the imagination to beyond the credible!

Thus, not everyone, evidently, was prepared at the time to concur with this 'disingenuous interpretation' of recent Austrian history. For a start, it would be to overlook the fact that just before the end of World War 2, Austrian Communists were plotting with the Soviet Union to 're-establish' Austria as a puppet-Communist state. On 29 March 1945 the Soviet commander Fyodor Tolbukhin's troops crossed the former Austrian border at *Klostermarienberg* in Burgenland. On 3 April, at the beginning of the Vienna Offensive, the Austrian politician Karl Renner, then living in southern Lower Austria, established contact with the Soviets. Joseph Stalin had already established a would-be future Austrian cabinet from the country's communists-in-exile, but Tolbukhin's telegram changed Stalin's mind in favor of Renner. One-third of State Chancellor Renner's cabinet was staffed by Austrian Communists. The Western allies suspected the usual Soviet pattern of setting up puppet states and did not recognize Renner. The British were particularly hostile; even the

American political leader Harry Truman, who believed that Renner was a trustworthy politician rather than a token front for the Kremlin, denied him recognition. But Renner had secured inter-party control by designating two Under-Secretaries of State in each of the ministries, appointed by the two parties. Consider now the work of Simon Wiesenthal, a well-known Jewish Austrian campaigner and writer, and the so-called `Nazi-Hunter'. He had for some time been investigating the past of **Kurt Waldheim**. It seems that this was upsetting the `Establishment' to such an extent that, in 1983 and in 1986 he had failed to be nominated for the Nobel Peace Prize, which he had been hoping for. As Secretary General of the World Jewish Congress [WJC] in 1989, Israel Singer explained to Wiesenthal that "Hunters don't win peace prizes." Nearing the end of October, 1989, after Kurt Waldheim had strenuously denied that he, as an SS officer, had authorised the deportation of Jews in Salonika, the WJC President, Rabbi Hertzberg said that `the world would be better served' if Waldheim did not stand for re-election to the Austrian Presidency:

....*"The problem of Waldheim is the problem of Austria. It is no longer the problem of the World Jewish Congress. We have spoken our last word on the subject."*

Perhaps the lesson to be learnt here is that we shouldn't court favours from the Establishment, wherever we may live, because that would be to grant them more power than would otherwise be due to them!

Now, the `exciting' thing about `surfing the net' is that you never know what surprises are in store when you undertake searches, and so it was, though in an increasingly macabre-sense, that I had been directed to a database of Austrian Holocaust Victims in the on-line document entitled *"Recht als Unrecht: Quellen zur wirtschaftlichen Entrechtung der Wiener Juden durch die NS-*

Vermogensverkesstelle," published by the *Osterreichisches Staatsarchiv* [i.e., the Austrian State Archive]. Of course, I searched the alphabetically-ordered long list with a mixture of excitement and trepidation until I arrived at `HALPERN', because, for me, this was a tentative step in the dark.

To cut a long story short, I did find the name of a person there who might have been my late mother's mum, noted her date of birth and her list-number ["zahl"], and duly wrote a letter to this effect to the Austrian State Archives in Vienna. At this stage I was unsure because, although I knew that my mum's brother was called Hans, I had not found `Hans Halpern' on the list. I duly added my name and that of my brother John to the letter, together with mum's date of birth and details of her death. The wheels of any civil service department in any country always grind slowly, but eventually I received a reply confirming that this lady that I had noted on the data base really was my late mother's mum, and I was given some gruesome information as to her fate and that of her son, mum's older brother Hans. Armed with this piece of information, I was able to email the IKG (*Israelitischen Kultusgemeinde*) in Vienna - which I had by now discovered was the organisation which had represented the Jewish populace of Vienna [and indeed the whole of Austria] - and then, little by little, was able to form a picture of my late mother's family in Vienna. The IKG were extraordinarily helpful and patient, and were able to draw upon their considerable array of records and other sources of information to inform me of details such as: where my mother and her family lived, when my mum had left Vienna for England, when her father had died and was buried, how old he was, where he came from, my mum's brother's age, my maternal grandmother's parents' names and her aunty's name. Then there were the details which I had already prepared myself to hear from them: the destination concentration-camps of my maternal `grandmother' and my mum's older brother and the dates of the `trains' that they took their last journey on. And all of this emailing to-and-fro had of necessity to be in English because, due mainly to my own laziness, I had neglected to learn German. French would not have been a problem, because I have a working knowledge of the language. But not German!

I kept my brother informed of what I was discovering at every stage, so that we were both beginning to fully recognise our true identity. Furthermore, at around this time, there was a large lawsuit being filed in the US courts against certain of the Austrian/German banks that had allegedly been complicit in the 'theft' of huge sums of money from the bank accounts of victims of National Socialism. The fact that the lawsuit was withdrawn a year or two later was not of great consequence to us because it was 'speculative', and I was not sure what degree of support, if any, it had from the US Government, the UK Government and those of other Western-, Eastern- and Central-European Governments. Anyhow, by now I had registered our names as potential claimants with the *General Settlement Fund for Victims of National Socialism*, set up by the Austrian Government, since John and I believed that we were the sole surviving relatives of our 'maternal grandmother' in the matter of the theft of her estate by the Nazis (i.e., National Socialists) during the Second World War. If nothing else, then we would hopefully discover a little more about mum's side of the family. The Executive Committee and the research/implementation team of this Settlement Fund, comprising an army of lawyers and administrators, chaired by an eminent international barrister and supported by a team of specialists pertaining to modern Austria, were appointed. They were assigned the task of allocating a fixed sum of money approved by the Austrian Government, and which was, by the Government's own admission, token compensation to surviving Austrian victims and surviving relatives of deceased Austrian victims. In this way, John and I were able to ascertain the nature and extent of our 'grandmother Anna Halpern's savings and investments, as well as to discover that, apparently, she did not own the flat that she and her family had seemingly lived in for many years after her marriage, and which was our late mother's childhood home.

This series of steps by the Austrian Government was a significant breakthrough for Austrian survivors and surviving relatives of the Austrian victims, because the Austrian Government has for a long while struggled to admit the extent of `systemic anti-Semitic sympathy that continues to pervade Austria'. Thus it had not been easy for the Austrian Government to vote through the monies involved, albeit that the sum was not large, relatively speaking. After World War II, a considerable time-span was needed for Austria to `officially' take responsibility for its actions in relation to its Jewish population both in the run-up to the Second World War and during that War. I say `officially' because anti-Semitism is still acknowledged as being prevalent amongst a significant proportion of that nation's population. What is more, nearly none found it worth the effort to invite the 'Jewish émigrés' to return to their homeland from May 1945 onwards.

Only in the 1980s did people begin to rethink and reflect upon public opinion. And only in July 1991 did the Austrian government compose a statement, communicated by *Bundeskanzler* [Federal Chancellor] Varanitzky to the Austrian Parliament and which acknowledged Austria's participation in the crimes of the *Third Reich*. However we had to wait nearly ten years on from that date, in January 2001, before the Republic of Austria and the USA signed the Washington Agreement, which lay *"the foundation for several vital steps in the belated process of coming to terms with National Socialism in Austria"* and provided for the establishment of the General Settlement Fund, the compensation of seized tenancy rights by the National Fund and the upcoming restoration of the Jewish cemeteries in Austria. In a speech that the Director-General of the Fund, Dr. Hannah Lessing, gave on its tenth anniversary, she noted that Franz Wahle, a member of the Fund's Arbitration Panel and a guest at the event, had been a child-participant of the traumatic war-time *Kindertransport* scheme. She added that he had at first rightly been very sceptical about whether Austria was willing to deal with its National Socialist past, and continued *"Although we are today still constantly aware of the fact that nothing can be set right, I hope that Karl Wahle would have viewed the work of the Arbitration Panel and its contribution towards a belated attempt at `Wiedergutmachung` [`reparation`] favourably."*

So what was the situation in mum's Austria in early May, 1945, a few days before I was born?

Upon the acceptance of defeat by the Germans in May, 1945, if not before, German presence in Eastern Europe was thus abruptly terminated. A new world- order was now taking shape, dominated by the Soviet Union. Nearly two million Poles were compulsorily transferred from eastern areas of Poland that had been annexed by the USSR. They took the place of Germans expelled from the formerly German regions of Pomerania and Silesia, now transferred to Poland. Half a million Ukrainians, Belarusians and others were deported from Poland to the Soviet Union. Hundreds of thousands of Ukrainians, Estonians, Latvians, Lithuanians, Croats, and others, fearful of reprisals for wartime collaboration, fled westwards from all over eastern Europe, most of them hoping to get to North America. **The willingness of the Ukranians to aid and abet the Nazis in their slaughter of the Jewish populations in the Ukraine and Poland, was seemingly coming back to haunt them. But this is another part of my story........**

Unbelievably, post-war anti-Semitic *Pogroms* broke out in Poland and Slovakia, in which Jews were killed. Over 100,000 Jews infiltrated to the western powers' zones in Germany and Austria. Most sought permission to enter Palestine - but the British mandatory government in Palestine denied entry to all save a handful. These Jews therefore remained stuck for years in so-called *displaced persons' camps*.

IKG Wien [Viennese Jewish Community] estimates that approximately 15,000 Jews are living in Austria today, most of them in Vienna. Furthermore, during the 2001 census, only 8140 Jews in Austria were counted, since not all wanted to declare openly that they were Jewish. This is not surprising, given that surviving Jews from concentration camps who returned to their homes found that they were unwelcome. Their property had new occupants, though [leading] questions as to how they came into ownership/occupation of this property will probably meet with evasive answers. And, unsurprisingly, the new incumbents were generally reluctant to vacate the premises. Yet the anger and frustration of Greek-Cypriot owners of property taken over by Turkish invaders of 1974 during the seizing of the northern part of Cyprus palls into insignificance in comparison to the fate of the majority of disinherited Viennese Jews, who did not even survive to confront those who somehow `came into ownership' of their property.

The notion of `national responsibility' referred to by Austrian Federal Chancellor Varanitzky and Dr Lessing above, alludes to the degree of support among the Austrian populace for the enforced *Anschluss* imposed by National Socialist Germany, which joined Austria politically with Germany.

In his reflective but candid `*Unsentimental Journey to Vienna: A Native Jew's Welcome Home'*, Benno Weiser offers an insider's view, glimpsed through the eyes of a native who came to renounce Austria and was, as a Jew, renounced by his `homeland.' He writes *"I was born [circa 1914] in the Austrian empire...... In 1918 my birthplace became part of Rumania. I began my career as a refugee at the age of nine months. My father was in the army, and my mother was unable to take both of her children with her in her departure from my native Czernovitz for Austria proper, so my grandmother, then visiting us, took me along when she returned to Poland. I was* *restored to my family in Vienna two years later, and had acquired in the meantime two grandmother tongues, Polish and Yiddish. I forgot Polish very soon and later had to re-learn Yiddish, but both left their mark on my early German. I was teased about my intonation by classmates and teachers, and straightened it out in later years. But I never adopted the Viennese dialect. I wanted to speak impeccable German, but stubbornly refused to disguise myself in order to be taken for Viennese-born—or anything other than the Jew I was……. ." As it happened, Jews in those days felt more secure in Germany than in Austria. There had long been a Judenfrage [`Jewish Problem'] in Austria, though between 1918 and the rise of Nazism it was by no means oppressive: if in Rumania and Poland anti-Semitism could be compared with T.B (i.e. Tuberculosis)., in the Austria of those years it amounted to no more than a chronic cold………… . In 1943, in Ecuador, I applied for a travel document for foreigners. Under the rubric "Nationality," the Ecuadorian official filled in "German." I protested. . . .*

"Why do you deny being German? (he retorted):after all, you have an expired German passport!"

"It was forced on me," I responded. "My homeland was invaded. I am Austrian."

The man looked at me sympathetically and said, "Austria doesn't exist any longer. Where were you born?"

"Let's not get into that," I implored; "it will only complicate matters ..."

With the Occupying Powers' arrangements for Austria in 1945, formal peace had come to Austria and, with it, sovereignty. It therefore became more important than ever for me to understand the country where the soul of such a large part of the recent Jewish past lies buried.

15 FATHOMING LOYALTY AND DEPRAVITY

'll recap a little to assist in adding more detail to my picture. The *Anschluss* had led quickly to the methodical and systematic persecution, and ultimately the genocide of a huge proportion of Austria's Jewish population, my 'would-be grandma and uncle' and maybe other Austrian relatives included. Jewish organizations and institutions were coercively disbanded and stripped of their assets, and with the establishment of the National Socialist's **euphemistic** *"Zentralstelle für jüdische Auswanderung"* ("centre for Jewish emigration") in the summer of 1938, the forced 'mass-emigration' [i.e. deportation to concentration-camps] was placed in its organizational framework, the ultimate objective of which was the total extermination of European Jews [i.e., the *Shoah*].

The purpose of the *Wannsee Conference*, held in Berlin in January, 1942, was to 'rubber-stamp' what had by then been termed the *'Final Solution'*, a code name for the systematic, deliberate, physical annihilation of the European Jews. At some still undetermined time in 1941, Hitler had authorized this European-wide scheme for mass murder. Heydrich convened the Wannsee Conference to inform them that he had been chosen by Hitler to co-ordinate the implementation of this operation. Most participants were already aware that the National Socialist regime had engaged in mass murder of Jews and other civilians in the German-occupied areas of the Soviet Union and in Serbia. Some of the actions were known to *Einsatzgruppen* and other police and military units, which were already slaughtering tens of thousands of Jews in the German-occupied Soviet Union. Others knew that units of the German Army and the SS and police were killing Jews in Serbia. There was unanimous approval at the Conference to the 'Final Solution' policy that Heydrich announced. Leaving their homes and possessions behind, more than 130,000 Jews managed to escape by the end of

October 1941, in many cases with the financial support of international Jewish organizations and the organizational assistance of the Jewish community. Yet about 16,000 of them were again caught and `deported' later on by their persecutors in other [German-captured] European countries. . Upon conclusion of the mass-deportations from Vienna by October 1942, the National Socialist `rulers' of Austria had already transported more than 47,000 Jews to ghettos, extermination camps and other sites of extermination; and until 1945, further deportations followed. Altogether more than 65,500 Jews from Austria were eliminated in the Shoah. In Austria only approximately 5,500 Jews survived, most of them due to so-called *"Mischehen"* (intermarriages).

Yet the seeds of National Socialism had been present among a considerable proportion of the Austrian populace for years before Austria's annexation to Nazi- controlled Germany. At school in Austria, Poetsch was Hitler's teacher from first - to- third grade (1901–04) in geography, and in second and third grade in history. He also ran the school library.

Hitler became enamoured of Poetsch as a teenager, captivated by the professor's fiery speeches and teachings, and began reading a local anti-Semitic newspaper regularly. Poetsch was a fervent pan-German who, by definition, sought to bring together all German-speaking populations of Europe so as to form a nation-state called Greater Germany. Poetsch despised the Hapsburgs and forcefully argued that all ethnic Germans should be united by a single government. Like many Austro-Germans, Poetsch wanted to see the old empire fall apart, with Austria then joining Germany, to the north. He asserted that the Aryan race was stronger, healthier, and fitter to rule than any other people. Poetsch declared that Jews and Slavs were what he termed "inferior races". (This position was not uncommon among impoverished Germans after World War I.) Hitler stated that *"Poetsch used our budding nationalistic fanaticism as a means of educating us, frequently appealing to us our sense of national honour."* Under Poetsch, Hitler came to the realization that:

"Germanism could be safeguarded only by the destruction of Austria, and, furthermore, the national sentiment is in no sense identical with dynastic patriotism; that above all, the House of Hapsburg was destined to be the misfortune of the German national." Von List, another of Hitler's luminaries, died in 1919, but his teachings survived through the National Socialists and it became mandatory for SS officers to learn the occult meanings of the Runic symbols.

At the end of the First World War, Hitler was developing his ideology, and his dislike of the Communist régime, now establishing itself as the USSR, was matched by his fascination with the Occult and of propaganda that portrayed all Jews as stereotypical money-grabbing lenders. He was now associating himself with groups that excluded anyone unable to demonstrate their `pure Germanic' derivation, which was to provide the foundation of the Nazis' anti-Semitic policies.

The occult has been defined as supernatural beliefs or phenomena; furthermore, Occult circles had reportedly long been known as covers for espionage and influence-peddling. Students of the post-First World War have periodically been warned not to underestimate occultism's influence on Hitler, apparently notwithstanding his subsequent rejection of Free Masons and esoteric movements.

A great deal has been speculated in relation to the links between the formulation of the **Aryan** principle for the establishment of the pure Germanic race, the connection between the so-called Aryans and the Teutons, and their belief that Freemasons and Jewish bankers were being led by a `God' hell-bent on war and destruction. In the eyes of the *Thulegesellschaft*, from which later emerged the DAP (German Worker's Party) and the SS (Schutzstaffel), the Jewish people who had supposedly been charged by the Old Testament *God* JAHVEH to "raise havoc on Earth" were the reason why the world was always caught up in war and discord. The Thule people felt it was their task to fight the Jewish people, and especially their banking and lodge system, and to `erect the realm of light upon Earth.' Yet I would hold that in so believing, they were relinquishing self-responsibility and handing it over to Satan. Their hatred was making them so blinded that they were in effect becoming slaves of Satan rather than acknowledging and following the peace-loving Son of God, Jesus.

Whilst Hitler's spying set-up, under Canaris and Heydrich was well aware of espionage channels, particularly from the direction of Britain and its *MI5* intelligence agency [the *"Occult Bureau"*], and whilst these potential sources of trouble were purged from Nazi life, that did not necessarily mean that Hitler and the Nazi secret societies were uninfluenced by mystical and occult writers. These would have included Blavatsky, Rudolf Steiner and Theodor Fritsch, and whilst Hitler later denounced and ridiculed many of them, he did dedicate his book *Mein Kampf* to his pan-Germanic teacher-mentor Dietrich Eckart. But General Karl Haushofer, a university don and director of the Munich Institute of Geopolitics was by now in extended discussions with Hitler and Adolf Hess. Haushofer's geophysical theories – on Germany swallowing up Slavic state to give it some `living space' - were welcomed by Hitler, and such was his influence on the Führer's thinking that, as esoteric mentor, Haushofer replaced Eckart. And we should note here that Steiner [whose name is linked to a number of schools in the UK] was a well-known Freemason and that most of Steiner's lectures on Freemasonry are included in two volumes: *Temple Legend*, and *Occult Brotherhoods*.

Many Christians might interpret the `occult doctrine', which Hitler and his supporters 'followed' and put into practice in such a deadly fashion, as just one form of outward expression of the `powers and principalities' referred to Ephesians 6:12 of the New Testament. The New International Version of the Bible [NIV] puts it like this:

"For our struggle is not against flesh and blood, but against the rulers, against the authorities, against the powers of this dark world and against the spiritual forces of evil in the heavenly realms."

Paul the Apostle's journey from being Saul of Tarsus, a young Jewish religious fanatic throwing himself into the fight to destroy Christ to becoming one of the most passionate of Christ's apostles, was so amazing that it is likely not to be overlooked even in modern Jewish religious teaching circles.

Yet, Chapter 53 of Old Testament's Book of Isaiah is omitted from their Torah because it prophesied that Christ was the Messiah who God gave to mankind, and that he would be killed by the Jews only to be resurrected after three days. Thus, Apostle Paul's personal journey apart, many Jews have not been prepared to accept that Christ, as the Son of God, **is** the saviour of Israel because they believe that the Messiah has yet to come and that he will be a warrior-king who will protect Israel. Yet Jewish Christians and Messianic Jews, who believe in the truth of Isiah 53, accept their Messiah as being Christ, and that he has already come not only to save Israel but to save all of mankind and to bring about peace and harmony between peoples. For anyone in my late mother's family circle of the 1920s in Vienna, to have broached this subject would have meant seriously risking their reputation as Jewish individuals, and the same would have been true in Jewish New York circles 30-50 years on.

Jewish commentators have argued like this: centuries of Jewish isolation followed the temple's destruction in A.D. 70 and led to deep introspection on the part of Israel's scholars. That led to a re-evaluation of Isaiah 53. Whereas the prophet Isaiah anticipated a hopeful peoples' search for Messiah, medieval scholarship reflected a suffering peoples' loss of perspective. Whereas Isaiah's forecast brightened Israel's future, relentless cycles of medieval religious and secular pogroms bludgeoned it. Unwilling to blame their rejection of the Messiah that Isaiah 53 anticipated, Israel's sages internalized the prophet to fit the historical situation as they experienced it, not as their Jewish ancestors foresaw it. Since it's easier to blame others, including God, for miseries our mistakes inflict on us and others, however, the 'medievalist' view remains the dominant Jewish position today.

So what, my readers might ask, has this passage from Isaiah got to do with my late mother's life and, for that matter, with the Holocaust? I readily confess not to being an expert in reconciling the Jewish psyche and Jewish faith with the outworking of the Holocaust. However, I would suggest that while the passage of time clarifies the meaning of historical events, it may also prejudice our overview of those events. Thus, people today believe that present-day Israel lives in the shadow of past persecution, not in the hope of future deliverance. Israelis' introspection and preoccupation with their past cannot offer a more accurate interpretation of Isaiah 53 than that of earlier generations of Israelite scholars.

Pogroms, which are planned campaigns of persecution or extermination, have been a feature of the lives of European Jews over many centuries; but what was emerging in Austria as well as other parts of Europe was particularly ominous. Even as far back as 1919, the Austrian Social Democrats formed the majority of those in Austria who wanted the *Anschluss*, which was the implementation of the merger of Germany with Austria. After Hitler's rise to power, this merger became less attractive, but in July, 1934, Austrian Nazis and their German counterparts together attempted a *coup d'état*, but were unsuccessful. An authoritarian right-wing Government then took power in Austria, and this authoritarianism prevented up to half of the country's population from voicing its legitimate dissent, such that the political split in Austria prevented concerted resistance to the developments in 1938. Hitler was using his Austrian Nazi allies as puppets in his bullying tactics, and when Hitler's wishes met with resistance from Austria's leadership, right up to the point when President Miklas refused to appoint Austrian Nazi leader Seyss-inquart as chancellor, Germany invaded the country on March 12th, 1938. The ensuing enthusiasm which met this invasion gave Hitler the cover to annex Austria the day after, and a controlled plebiscite of April 10th gave a 99.7% approval to this move.

On the 12th and 13th of March, 1938, Nazi troops entered Austria, which, at the time, had a Jewish population of 200,000. Hitler simultaneously announced **Anschluss** [union] with Austria. The SS was placed in charge of Jewish affairs in

Austria, with Adolf Eichmann establishing an Office for Jewish Emigration in Vienna. Himmler then established Mauthausen concentration camp near Linz.

Seen in retrospect, Mum's departure from Vienna came in the lead-up to declaration of war, with the Germans' policy on Jews shifting from enthusiasm for shifting the Jewish population out of Europe to one set fair on total extermination of the European Jewry. From the Nazi capture of power in Germany in 1933, the main thrust of Germany's Jewish policy was initially one of facilitating outward migration; the German government had thence introduced a series of laws, the cumulative result of which was to comprehensively exclude Jews from the civic- and economic-life of Germany. The German government had even gone as far as to be a party to a special arrangement with the Jewish Agency for Palestine which saw forty or so thousand Jews emigrate from Germany to Palestine between 1933 and 1938, alongside provisions to allow the departing Jews to take some [albeit a reducing part] of their financial assets with them in return for trading- and currency- concessions on the part of the Palestine Authority. And in August, 1938, a Central Office for Jewish Migration was established in Vienna under the auspices of the Gestapo. Mum had, however, already left her Austrian homeland by then, having announced her departure for England on 9th June, 1938. This was a move which, whilst saving her own life, left her mother and brother alone as prey to the Nazi murderers and their Austrian collaborators. How she obtained a permit to leave the country in June, 1938 I can only venture at. She was just over 19 years of age, and almost certainly too old to have joined the *Kindertransport*. Furthermore, at that point in time, it was becoming increasingly difficult for Jewish people to leave Austria after the *Anschluss*, not to mention other Western, Central- and Eastern European states which had been over-run and incorporated into the German *Reich*. Britain carried a great deal of responsibility in this respect, not only in respect of controlling entry of Jews into Britain, but also in relation to its enforcement of a `forcible' immigration-control policy as `administrator' of the British Mandate in Palestine. Huge numbers of Jewish Europeans were desperately trying to flee to Palestine. The Zionists in Britain and the United States were not only desperately trying to persuade their own governments to permit more Jews right of entry to Britain and the US respectively , but also to be instrumental in the designation of a new Jewish State occupying land which presently lay within the boundaries of Palestine.

In this latter regard, they faced outright objection from the Arabs, who were able to hold sway in terms of British policy. The British Government had drawn up the crucial pre-war White Paper which set out their policy in relation to ruling between the Arabs and the Jews in Palestine. This document did not support partition of the Palestinian territory, nor did it envisage the creation of an independent Jewish state. Instead it put its weight behind the concept of power-sharing. Mindful of the strategic economic- and political importance of the Suez Canal, and conscious of the extent of growth of Jewish land-ownership in Palestine, it wished to maintain the *status quo* in the Near-and Middle East, especially in those territories where it still exercised its colonial power. The majority holding sway in the British Government, alongside its Civil Service back-up, was not prepared to put its weight behind the Jewish cause, but, on the contrary, supported the Arabs. It was playing a difficult power-game on the world-stage, arguably seeming to want to appease the Arabs in these territories in relation to this delicate issue. It had therefore stuck rigorously to this White [policy] Paper, leaving Winston Churchill facing an uphill battle in this respect, both as Lord of the Admiralty at the outbreak of the Second World War and subsequently as Prime Minister. Churchill was as vehemently pro-Zionist as his political colleagues were anti-, but was consistently over-ruled both by his fellow Wartime Cabinet members and by Civil Servants both here in

Westminster and in the [British-controlled] Palestine-Government. They were unconvinced by the argument that their anti-Zionist stance would alienate the US administration at a time when Britain needed US support in its war effort, although it was acknowledged that the American public did not necessarily equate the suffering Jewish people with the articulate and vociferous Zionist movement. The Zionists had sought to gain control of representative Jewish organisations in Britain, but this only served to increase the determination of anti-Zionists in power to refuse to budge on their Jewish immigration policy. The growing number of Jewish immigrants settling in Palestine was tipping the Jewish/Arab population-balance so greatly that the British Cabinet of the time chose to 'put a brake' on it by shutting the doors of Britain and Palestine to the flood of Jews seeking safe refuge, one of the consequences of which was to entrap a huge number of European Jews in the German Reich, and therefore to almost certain death through shooting/gassing in the growing number of concentration camps being set up across Poland and Belorussia, etc. by the Nazi regime. As Bernard Wasserstein put it in his book *"Britain and the Jews of Europe, 1939-1945"*, "Upon the outbreak of war these principles froze into axioms of official decision making, and so it continued until the end of the war..." The Nazis were keeping their anti-Semitic atrocities across Europe so secretive that those who actually knew what was going on and were possibly in a position to draw the world's attention to the horrific reality of the situation, were finding it extremely dangerous and difficult to get the news out, even risking their lives. Even when the scant news of the unfolding tragedy of the Jews at the hands of the Nazis did surface, it was not acted upon sufficiently in political circles in Britain. To add to the misery of the Jewish cause, the likes of William Joyce, a.k.a *Lord Haw-Haw*, were lending their weight to the Big Lie which Hitler's misinformation/ propaganda machine was actively disseminating across the radio waves of Europe, especially Britain.

In relation to the movement of Jews, what we are talking about here are the roots of the capitalized *Diaspora*, i.e. the Jewish diaspora. We have seen the Arab opposition to the arrival of Jews in Palestine during the Second World War and this contributed to colonial rule and to the establishment of the state of Israel. The Middle Eastern nations were to translate that into hostility towards their historic Jewish populations of about one million people [*the Sephardim*], with most of these Jews emigrating, mainly to Israel, where they became known as the *Mizrahi Jews*.

The flip side of the coin is that the uncapitalised word 'diaspora' [i.e. population dispersion in a general sense] can mean immigrant- or refugee-populations settling away from their established or ancestral homelands, such as the *Palestinian diaspora* of 1948, which came about after the attempt to dismantle Israel, and saw three-quarters of a million Palestinians being displaced from their former territory.

In the time leading up to World War Two, Hitler was spending a lot of time at his Bavarian mountain retreat of Berghof. Pre-war guests had numbered political figures, monarchs, heads of state and diplomats along with painters, singers and musicians. David Lloyd George had visited the retreat in early March, 1936, the Aga Khan on the 20th October, 1937, the Duke and Duchess of Windsor on the 22nd of that same month and Neville Chamberlain on September, 1938. Prince Edward had abdicated the British throne a mere nine months before becoming Hitler's guest at Berghof, by which time he had married the American divorcee Wallis Simpson and he and his wife had been granted the titles Duke and Duchess of Windsor. What are we to read into this visit of the Windsors?

Mum was sparing in comments relating to politics and the royalty, but I do recall her remarking to me as a teenager that there was sympathy amongst a certain element of the British royalty before/during the war to the Nazi cause. She did not elaborate, and, anyhow, I was too pre-occupied with other things to give it more thought at the time. Besides which, mum always wished to instill in us the value of patriotism. However, given mum's monitoring work at the BBC during the war, she had good reason to make that remark, which seems to draw some credence from the following observations:

a] Queen Victoria's mother tongue was German] Following the First World War, the royal family changed its name from *Saxe-Coburg-Gotha* to *Windsor* to deflect attention from its German heritage;

c] The Nazis were reputed to have intended installing the aforesaid Duke of Windsor as leader and `King' of a German Britain after a successful conquest of that country;

d] Baron Gunther Hubertus von Reibnitz (of German descent), was the father of Princess Michael of Kent [a.k.a Baroness Marie Christine Anna Agnes Hedwig Ida; *née* von Reibnitz; born 15.01.1945). The Baron was a party member and an honorary member of the SS several weeks before Germany invaded Poland]. Prince Michael is a cousin of Queen Elizabeth II of the United Kingdom;

e] King George VI and his wife, the late Queen Mother, allegedly sent Hitler a birthday greeting;

f] Family members of Queen Elizabeth's husband Prince Philip, who is from the house of Schleswig-Holstein-Sonderburg-Glucksburg, were said to be unabashed supporters of Hitler and the Nazis; furthermore, brother-in-law, Prince Christoph of Hesse, was a member of the SS. He piloted fighters that attacked Allied troops in Italy.

My late mother considered it important to instill the sense of **national loyalty** into both my brother and I, so the burning question which all the aforesaid statements beg me to ask is `Does the deliberate identification of individuals with a group sworn to secrecy in relation to its proceedings and certain of its activities, run counter to loyalty in society in *general, and especially as it pertained to the seemingly distinct pro-Nazi leaning of Britain's royal family at the time?'*

Suffice it to say that as recently as 2013, HRH Prince Michael of Kent was **Provincial Grand Master of the Provincial Grand Lodge of Middlesex.** Furthermore, HRH the Duke of Kent was **Grand Master of the United Grand Lodge of England** in the same year, and Prince Philip is what is known as a **1st degree Freemason.** I have never had the inclination to be anything more than reliably informed about Freemasonry, and in this vein I had noted being informed some years back by a former acquaintance – apparently an erstwhile Freemason - that he had to lie in a coffin as part of his initiation into the Masonic Lodge. Apparently, in the third degree of initiation, the initiate is blind folded and led around by a noose around his neck. In this degree the initiate is approached by three ruffians who demand the initiate to tell them the secrets of Hiram Abiff. Hiram Abiff is the legendary builder of Solomon's temple and founder of Freemasonry. The person leading the initiate speaks for him and refuses to tell the three ruffians, so they proceed to symbolically beat him to death. **He is then placed into a coffin or stretcher in a symbolic burial.** This evidently invites in a spirit of death. After a while the worshipful Master of the Lodge directs a person with a glove that resembles a lion's paw, to reach down and pull the initiate out of the darkness of death and into the light of freemasonry. True Christians would regard this ritual as being an absolute mockery of the death, burial and resurrection of Jesus Christ.

Having now briefly offered some admittedly very sketchy notes on the position of Britain's ruling monarchy in relation to Hitler, both prior to and during the Second World War, I shall now try to set alongside these notes a summary of the Government's stance on allowing Jewish refugees to enter the country and its 'colonies' during the 1930s and in the run-up to the Second World War.

In line with its complex history, Britain was not that keen to permit accepting Jewish refugees fleeing the Nazi regime in Germany and other European Fascist states. However, approximately 40,000 Jews from Austria or Germany were eventually allowed to settle in Britain **before the War**, in addition to 50,000 Jews from Italy, Poland and elsewhere in Eastern Europe. The Evian Conference held in France in 1938 proved a failure because both the United States and Britain refused to accept substantially more refugees, and most of the countries at the Conference followed suit, the result being that the Jews had no escape and were ultimately subject to what was known as Hitler's *"Final Solution to the Jewish Question"*. The Conference was thus seen by some as "an exercise in Anglo-American collaborative hypocrisy." With the declaration of war, 74,000 German, Austrian and Italian citizens in the UK were interned as enemy aliens. After individual consideration by tribunal, the majority, comprising Jewish and other refugees, were released within six months. Did mum have to go before that tribunal, then to be released within 6 months? The other question that I have to ask myself is `did mum ever hope [against hope?] that her mother and brother would be able to follow in her footsteps and make their way to Britain?' Or at least make it to the shores of the United States in the first instance?

All I know now is that mum was to contact the International Red Cross in Geneva, Switzerland in 1945, the year of my birth, and I believe that she even travelled there from London. Understandably, she wanted to know about the fate of her mother and brother, yet, at no point while mum was alive did she ever tell us about what she learnt. How did this news affect her from that point on? And did it influence her behaviour and affect her relationship with dad from that point onwards? Suffice it to say here that when Anthony Eden became Prime Minister in post-war Britain, I was too young and innocent to appreciate the significance of his rôle in government in preventing Jewish refugees entering Britain at the outbreak of the Second World War.

I am indebted to Lisa Thier, a good friend of the family who grew up in Friedrichshafen and works as a young doctor in Germany, for her determined efforts in 2002 to dig out information pertaining to my late mother and her family in Vienna. Lisa had travelled to Vienna with a friend in early summer 2002 and was able to visit the 2nd District in Vienna where my late mother had grown up. She also kindly translated a lot of German language emails and documents relating to my mum's side of the family which had hitherto baffled me.

My wife Lynne, my brother John and I had travelled to Vienna a year previously and largely on a fact-finding mission, especially as we had no idea of the nature of mum's childhood home. Nor did we know anything significant about her brother Hans and about her mum Anna's family, especially her older sister Elise Zimmer/Czimmer and her brother Hermann Bäck. We were thus in a position to give Lisa details of the Austrian side of my family, and she was in turn to gather information so much more easily than me because she was German! Lisa was able to establish that Hermann was a bank director before he died in 1929, and that his estate was passed on to Anna and Elise/Elisabeth. We also gave Lisa details of the shop on the ground-floor of my late mother's family flat and the name of the lady who ran the shop who I had earlier contacted via the internet. Lisa and her friend were therefore able to speak this this lady a year later and pose questions about the ownership of the block of flats during the war and about how the present owner of the apartment block somehow came to be in possession of this property. Lisa was then able to make contact with the owner, who, predictably, shied away from answering these questions!

How, the reader might well ask, were the Nazis in Germany able to implement their objectives so efficiently across their huge theatre of operations, not only in Austria, but across Western-, Central- and Eastern-Europe? The answer is twin-headed: firstly it needed the co-operation of its supporters and sympathisers, including not only a goodly proportion of the German populace but also a German manufacturing industry desperate to survive and delighted to produce armaments, etc.; secondly it enjoyed the co-operation of banks extending across national boundaries in 'laundering' stolen assets; and thirdly, it enlisted the critical help of the likes of the American IBM computer company in drawing up a database of the Jewish populace across Europe, which the Nazis were then able to employ to meet its deadly ends. IBM thus 'sold its soul', ostensibly for the sake of increased European sales of its computers, and Hitler was now armed with a 'deadly tool' as far as the destiny of the European Jewry of the time was concerned.

That said, I shall stay with my focus on Austria for the time-being, although my subsequent family researches were to take me beyond that country. For the Nazis were to begin rounding up the Jewish people from across Europe and not only using them as slave labour to support the war that it was waging with Britain and its Allies, but shipping them by the thousands to concentration [i.e. extermination]-camps dotted across central Europe, especially the Jews deemed not be of any worth in its war-effort. Furthermore, it was collecting the gold and silver jewellery and gold false-teeth and fillings taken from their victims and melting it down so that they could cash-in on its worth. The Nazis were also raiding the bank-accounts of these doomed people to steal monies, stocks and share lodged with them for safekeeping.....

The banks in Austria, Switzerland and elsewhere, including *Credit Suisse*, were willing participants in this looting-operation, and the assets in Anna Halpern's bank accounts, including shares, which were deposited in her bank account in Austria, were no exception. Lisa Thier was able to establish through interpreting Nazi- documents that I had retrieved from the Austrian State Archives and liaising with officials in Vienna, that Anna Halpern had mining shares deposited in the Hypotheken-Creditinstitut und Aktiongesellschaft ['Bank'], which were initially destined to be handed over to the Prussian State Bank, Hitler's central-coffers, but the document in question issued by German officials in 1943, instructs the *Hypotheken 'Bank'* to hold back from handing these shares over to the Prussian Bank. On 3rd December, 1942, the year of her death, it was reported that Frau 'Anna Sara Halpern' had a savings account and other assets, but Hitler's German financial department did not know whether to confiscate these or not. By the following 30th June, it was determined that these monies were, after all, to be confiscated. The *Hypotheken 'Bank'* in Austria was to be incorporated into the *Erste Bank* following the end of the war now and is now one of the bigger banks in Austria. To its credit, the Erste Bank did confirm to me by email that the *Hypotheken-Creditinstitut* was its predecessor during the war.

The historical interpretation of events in Austria and the wishes of the Austrian people post-First World War and post-Second World War, are always going to be subjective and dependent upon where the interpreters' aims and sympathies lie. I shall therefore try to relate events which are not in contention.

The Austro-Hungarian Empire had been allies of Germany before the First World War, but both states were on the losing side, and, as a result of the Versailles Treaty in 1919, the Austro-Hungarian Empire was disbanded and divided into many countries, so that areas formerly under Austro-Hungarian jurisdiction are today located within the borders of Austria, Bosnia, Croatia, the Czech Republic, Hungary, Italy, Poland, Romania, Serbia, Slovakia, Slovenia and the Ukraine. Austria had hitherto been seen as the homeland of German-speaking Austrians who hitherto had mainly ruled the Austro-Hungarian Empire and had Vienna as their capital. The Versailles Treaty had also seen the defeated Germany having to give up a considerable amount of its territories to France, Poland and others, as well as being forced to pay huge reparation sums to the victors for the damage inflicted upon them by Germany during the First World War.

Thus a disgruntled number of these German-speaking `Austrians', incited by Adolf Hitler as the most prominent of their kind, not only came to demand the incorporation of the newly independent `Austria' as part of Germany, but to seek revenge for the `punishment' inflicted upon Germany by the Allied victors; by this is meant the implementation of the Versailles Treaty, to which Germany had not, of course, been a signatory. The years of economic depression following the end of the First World War had world-wide ramifications, especially in Europe and the United States, the engine-houses of industry. This was particularly bad for Germany as the defeated power because economic recovery was going to be that much more difficult. Thirsty for power, Hitler had begun to emerge as a force to be reckoned with at around 1930, and was quick to pour scorn on the frail Weimer Republic which had run the country for a short while at this time. The Republic lacked the steely toughness and political astuteness which was needed to outwit the tactics of the Pretender Hitler and to retain the respect of the desperately poor German electorate. The people needed work and the restoration of their dignity, their national pride, and Hitler was quick to latch onto these things.

It was Georg Spitaler at *DOW Wien* who told me about the circumstances in which my mum's own mum Anna and brother Hans were to meet their deaths. Anna Halpern, born in Vienna on July 28th, 1880, was put on the Nazi's mass-deportation train to Ghetto Izbica/Poland on 5th June, 1942. Her son Hans Halpern, born in Vienna on June 20th, 1914, was deported to Maly Trostinec, near Minsk, on the 2nd June, 1942. Anna's deportation train was given the title *"Transport XXV, 5.6.1942 nach Izbica Gen. Gouv,"* and Hans's as *"Transport XXIV 2.6.1942 nach Minsk."* Anna and her family had lived in the 2nd District of Vienna known variously as the `Quartier juif', Leopoldstadt and `Matzoh Island'. It was the centre of Jewish life in Vienna for a very long time until the implementation of the mass extermination of European Jewry known variously as the `Shoah'/`Holocaust'/`Catastrophe'. And whilst there are far fewer Jews now living in Vienna, it is said that the district still retains that distinctly Jewish feel.

It is said that the reason why the Leopodstadt is also called **"Matzoh Island"** was that it was here where many Viennese Jews were gathered before their deportation to concentration camps in the course of the Holocaust. Today there is a **memorial site** at a school where this happened.

I found it appalling to discover how the end finally came for my late mother's nearest and dearest next-of-kin. The closest parallel that comes to mind is the end that Jesus met on the cross. I have read several of Dr. Martin Gilbert's books on the Holocaust and the events leading up to it, as well as Thomas Keneally's *"Schindler's Ark"*, plus other literature on the Shoah in Austria and the wider Holocaust. But, excellent as they are in describing the events leading up to the exterminations, how can they begin to reach inside the minds of the likes of Anna and Hans at the point where they are confronted with their last gasps of air? What had they, along with the six million or so other European Jewry done to deserve this? It is therefore not surprising that mum's chosen way of dealing with the memory was to draw a veil in front of it.

The description I have found of my `uncle' [i.e. mum's brother] Hans's Transport can be summarised as follows: In April 1942, the Head of the Security Police and the S.D. Reinhard Heydrich, visited Minsk [now in Belarus] in person, and informed Strauch, the local KdS [Commander of Security Police and SD (security service and political intelligence)] that the Jewish Transports from the West to Minsk, interrupted at the end of 1941, had to be resumed, and that from then on these Jews were to be killed immediately after arrival. *KdS (Kommandeur der Sicherheitspolizei)* were intermediate-level command structures of the Security Police.

Aspang station in Vienna had been the scene of mass Jewish departures since 1939, to destinations such as Lublin. In deliberations between (Adolf) Eichmann and his subordinates, it was confirmed that the euphemistically coined *'Resettlement operation to Poland'* would begin at 22.00 hours on October 20, 1939, with the first transport of 1,000 Jews fit for work, from the Aspang Rail Station in Vienna.' Of some significance is the fact that the composition of the transports was arranged by the Jewish Community of Vienna [as long as that remained possible.] This is the same IKG Wien that today represents the Jewish Community in Vienna and which has access to many of the files of Austrian Jewish victims of the Holocaust, and through whom I have been able to discover so much about the maternal side of my family. During the war, the IKG was obliged to work for the Nazis in Austria.

Now move the calendar forward 18 or so months to May 6th, 1942, and we see a deportation train with 998 Jewish men, women and children on board, leave *Vienna Aspang* Station for Minsk. The office of KdS *Minsk* had carried out extensive organisational preparations in order to be able to exterminate these people as quickly and efficiently as possible. The chosen place of execution, a small pine wood at a few kilometres distant from Maly Trostinec estate, was a former *kolkhose*, which the KdS took over in April 1942. A *kolkhose* was a collective farm in the Soviet Union. By keeping close contact with the main railway administration `Mitte' in Minsk through a special liaison officer, the KdS made sure of being informed well in advance of the exact arrival time of the transports. As a first preparatory step, big trenches were then dug, measuring up to 3m deep and 50m in length.

The subsequent executions followed a pattern, involving 80-100 personnel, including members of the Schutzpolizei and the Wafen-SS. The trains would arrive at Minsk's freight-train station at between 4 and 7a.m., with KdS officials supervising the disembarkation of Jewish passengers and their luggage. These passengers were then herded to an assembly point, where their money and valuables were taken from them. At this stage in proceedings, the KdS would select a few - between 20 and 50 people per transport – whom they deemed suitable for forced labour on the Trostinec estate [i.e. the concentration camp]. Finally, the remaining deportees were taken by lorry to the trenches which were situated about 18km away. This process remained unchanged for the first 8 transports, including that of Hans Halpern.

Whilst deportees from the first transport were shot directly at the trenches by up to 20 marksmen, from about the beginning of June `1942 onwards, "gasvans" were also used, of which the KdS had three at its disposal. In that case, the victims were crammed into the cars at the loading point, i.e., first on the terrain of the freight in Minsk, and later next to the concentration camp branch line in Maly Trostinec, and taken to the trenches. Only there were the exhaust tubes connected and the gas fed into the cars. Due to technical problems and frequent defects, but also because of the necessary and labour-intensive cleansing of the "gasvans" after each murder assignment, those "gasvans" were not in constant use, and with later transports, there were mass-shootings too. Given, however, that Hans Halpern was on the transport of June 2nd, 1942, it is quite likely that he was one of the first people to be "gassed" at Maly Trostinec. From May 6th, 1942 to October 1942, there were 8 transports carrying about 7,500 Viennese Jews to Maly Trostinec, in addition to several hundred Austrians taken from Theresienstadt. Only 17 people are known to have survived among the almost 9,000 Austrian Jews deported to Maly Trostinec.

Anna Halpern's *"deportation-transport"* to **Izbica**, in Nazi-occupied Poland on 5th June 1942 was the last of four deportation transports with 4,000 Jewish men, women and children aboard which had departed for Izbica from Vienna's Aspang Station. The village of Izbica lies about 18km south of the Kreisstadt Krasnystow in Lublin district, whose original population of about 6,000 was about 90% Jewish. As a result of deportations from other parts of Poland, from the `Protektorat' [Austrians among them], from the old `Reich' and from Vienna, the number of Jewish residents swelled at times to 12,000.

The ghetto was created in 1941, although the first transports of Jews from the German Reich started arriving there already in 1940. Izbica was the largest transit ghetto in the Lublin reservation with a death rate almost equal to that of the Warsaw Ghetto. *SS Hauptsturmfuhrer Kurt Engels,* known for his exceptional cruelty, served as its only commandant.

At first, the Izbica ghetto was not fenced in, and there were no sentries to prevent its `population' from leaving. The Jewish `residents' were, however forbidden on pain of strictest punishment to leave the `town' without a permit.

It is here in Izbca that my ancestor Anna Halpern may have come face to face with what could be described as Hitler's Jewish collaborators. These were Jews who, even though I guess they knew that their options were limited, were still prepared to `sell their souls' to the Führer by becoming members of the **Jewish Council in Izbica**, thinking perhaps that they might thereby survive at least for a little longer. This Council of 12 people at Izbica was appointed to carry out the orders of the German authorities. There will always be betrayals from within; you only have to think of Jesus and one of his 12 disciples, Judas Iscariot, to realise the fathomless wrong implicit in the very act of betrayal.

The deportees probably did not metaphorically sit down to a `Last Supper' with any of the Council of 12, and we don't know whether any of these 12 were at liberty to wriggle out of the `job', maybe by feigning serious illness. But I accept that even that would not have prevented Hitler's men from carrying out their dirty deeds. No one will know of the sense of utter betrayal that must have been felt by the detainees being 'supported' by the Council of 12, only to realise at the last minute that they had boarded death's train to what happened to be a place called Belzec.

In what was probably a move to make room for the batch of Austrian deportees who were arriving after March 24th, 1942, some 2,200 or so of the 'prisoners' already at Izbica were moved on to the Belzec extermination-camp. This move, in line with the *Wannsee* policy, was organised initially by the Jewish Council and under the pretext that this group' might thereby gain an improvement in their living conditions'.

The organisation of the transport to Belzec was taken over by the S.S. *Umsiedlungsstab* [euphemistically termed the 'resettlement unit'] in the summer of 1942, so it is very likely that Anna Halpern, part of the 5th June transport to **Izbica**, was one of those internees who was deported from Izbica to Belzec in the summer of 1942, under the eye of this 'resettlement unit'. The detainees no longer had the option of volunteering to leave Izbica, but were now being taken by force, and each departing group of Jews was accompanied by one NCO and 15 SS men, most of them Ukrainian volunteers. These group departures were almost always accompanied by maltreatment and shootings, and by now, Izbica seems to have become a 'waiting room' for the Belzec extermination camp, whose intake was determined by the capacity of the Belzec gas chambers. Of the more than 4,000 Austrian Jews deported from Izbica, not one survived.

So Anna was quite likely to have been herded onto the Belzec transport by a Ukrainian volunteer, whose language, she might have recognised as snippets of the Ukrainian tongue, if she was sufficiently *compos mentis* at that point in time and had ever picked up any Ukrainian language from her late husband Michel. It must have been like being hit by a 'double whammy': Michel Halpern, who had died at the age of 45 in Vienna in 1922, was a [German and probably Yiddish-speaking] Jew born in what had by now become part of the Ukraine, and there they were, the Ukrainian nationals who he had lived alongside him during his childhood and youth, now metaphorically *kowtowing* to the Führer.   We shall never know whether Anna had gleaned anything about the fate of fellow Jews – including, perhaps, some relatives on the Halpern side - in Mikel Halpern's home town of Bolechow prior to her being rounded-up in Vienna in 1942. She had probably been house-bound for a while before being herded into a cattle truck heading – maybe unknowingly – to her horrible death. Georg Spitaler at DOW Vienna considered that the Nazis and their Austrian collaborators had moved the Halpern family from one flat to another in the Jewish Quarter of Vienna prior to their death-journeys.

The poem *"Vultures"* by Chinua Achebe, superficially describes the love between two vultures that feed on the dead together ; this is then compared to the indulgent love a WW2 concentration camp Commandant has for his child, having returned home after a day spent murdering people. Aside from comparing Achebe's description with the reality of Anna Halpern's situation, I was also drawn to reflect upon the perverse gluttony, material indulgence and corruption of the Nazi Camp Commandants described in vivid detail in Thomas Keneally's book `Schindler's Ark'. And lastly I was drawn to consider the words of the poet Wilfred Owen, trying to convey something of the infinite horridness, utter futility and costly but ultimately questionable sacrifice of war. It didn't matter for me that Owen, in `Dolce et Decorum Est', was describing the First- and not the Second- World War:

> *".....If you could hear, at every jolt, the blood*
> *Come gargling from the froth-corrupted lungs,*
> *Obscene as cancer, bitter as the cud(12)*
> *Of vile, incurable sores on innocent tongues,*
> *My friend, you would not tell with such high zest*
> *To children ardent for some desperate glory,*
> *The old Lie; Dulce et Decorum est*
> *Pro patria mori."*

As for the family of Anna's sister Elise [Elisabeth] Zinner/Czinner [née Bäck], this is another part of the story. Elise was somewhat older than Anna, and married. She died in the early 1930s, and though her death was at a relatively young age, at least she did not have to go through the fate of her younger sister and her nephew. That said, I know nothing about Elise's Austrian relatives on her late husband's side.

A description of Anna Halpern's destination reads as follows:

"The Nazi authorities of the Free City of Danzig were compiling material about known Jews and Polish intelligentsia as early as 1936 and were also reviewing suitable places to build concentration camps in their area. Originally, Stutthof was a civilian internment camp under the Danzig police chief. In November 1941, it became a "labor education" camp, administered by the German Security Police. Finally, in January 1942, Stutthof became a regular concentration camp.

The original camp (known as the `old camp') was surrounded by barbed-wire fence. It comprised eight barracks for the inmates and a "kommandantur" for the SS guards, totaling 120,000 m². In 1943, the camp was enlarged and a new camp was constructed alongside the earlier one. It was also surrounded by electrified barbed-wire fence and contained thirty new barracks, raising the total area to 1.2 km² (0.5 sq. miles). A crematorium and gas chamber were added in 1943, just in time to start mass executions when Stutthof was included in the "Final Solution" in June 1944. Mobile gas wagons were also used to complement the maximum capacity of the gas chamber (150 people per execution) when needed"

I have also found *Shoah Database* records relating to the destination of two Zinners/Czinners recorded as coming from Vienna, who were deported to a concentration camp in North Germany/Poland: Friederike Czinner was born on 6th April,

1875, and her address prior to being arrested and deported to the Wein/Thereienstadt concentration camp, was Wien 2, Grosse Sperlgasse 32/17. Friederike's date of deportation is given as 22nd July, 1942, and her death is recorded as being nine months later, on 18th February, 1943. They might well have been related to Elise Zinner/Czinner.

16 FROM BOLECHOW TO VIENNA

Mum's dad Michel Halpern was already working in Vienna in 1911, the year when he married Anna, and at the outbreak of the First World War in 1914, mum's brother Hans was born. Mum was born in 1919, the year of the creation of the Versailles Treaty. This Treaty was to lead to the dissolution of the Austro-Hungarian Empire, and, I guess, the Railway Company which it had created. Michel Halpern was employed as an official for this Company, though I do not know what happened to Michel's job when this change occurred. What is certain, though, is that Michel was to die in early 1923, before mum had even reached the age of 4, leaving it to Anna to bring up Hans and little Josephine on her late husband's occupational pension and the family's savings and very modest investments.

Michel Halpern was born in January, 1877 in the town of Bolechow in *Eastern Galicia*, which, at the time, was part of the *Austro-Hungarian Empire*. It is probable that his family spoke Yiddish, and maybe German or Russian or Ukrainian: such had been the changes in national boundaries that affected Eastern Galicia over the centuries. Nevertheless, in 1787, by decree of the Austrian Emperor, all Jews within the Empire were required to adopt German surnames; and, whilst the Emperor also required the rabbi in each Jewish community to maintain registers of births, marriages, and deaths, the rule was often ignored up until 1848.

Michel's birthplace and year of birth were as much as I knew at first about mum's dad, and for this information I am indebted to Georg Spitaler, then representing the DÖW in Vienna. DÖW or DOEW is the *Documentation Centre of Austrian Resistance*, and has acted as a source of data on the victims of the Gestapo. I can't remember how I came across DOW, but I can only assume that I must have been surfing the net intensively and came across their web-page by chance. Furthermore, I later came to discover that Jewish BMD[i.e., Birth, Marriage, Death] records in Austria were a good deal more accessible to genealogists and enlightened laypeople than those in what is the present-day Ukraine, making Georg's job that much easier.

Surfing the internet was also to lead me to a web-site organisation called *JewishGen*, based in the United States and with access to genealogical information held by the Polish Government. In return for a smallish donation in American dollars, I was allocated a password which gave me access to their expanding database of people whose records were held in Warsaw, Poland.

I will never know whether mum got to know a great deal about her late dad's family in Bolechow and whether she ever got to visit this smallish town in Eastern Galicia, now forming the western part of modern-day Ukraine. Given that she was scarcely three years old when he died, her memories of him, if indeed there were any, must have been very limited.

I feel sure however that her dad's home in Bolechow was nothing like the apartment where she grew up in Vienna's 2nd District. When my wife Lynne, my brother and I travelled to Vienna in 2001, to seek out more details relating to mum's side of the family, we rented a first-floor apartment fairly centrally. The building must have dated from the late 19th century, and had the high ceilings and large rooms and large entrance hall area which surely must have been akin to the apartment that my late mum grew up in.

The small provincial town of Bolechow must have been a `different kettle of fish' as far as family homes are concerned. The town has two rivers, the Sukil and the Svicha, running through it before joining the Dniester, flanked by the Carpathian Mountains lying to the southwest. The town is on Ukraine Highway 10 between Dolnya and Stryj, with the capital, Kiev, approximately 300 km away in a west northwesterly direction, below the Carpathian Mountains.

Up until 1772, the town of Bolechow came under the administration of the *Polish-Lithuanian Commonwealth*, being the *Kingdom of Poland*. At the risk of boring my readers, I will summarise its governance from thereon in. The town was part of the Province of *Rus Voivodship*, and further broken down into the District of *L'wow* [*L'viv/Lemburg*]. From 1172-1867, it lay within the *Hapsburg Empire*, then part of the *Austrian Empire* from 1804. The Province of *Rus Voivodship* had by now become the *Kingdom of Galicia and Lodomeria*, and the district was now *Dolina powiat*. Whilst the town remained part of the same province and district until 1914, it was to lie within the *Austro-Hungarian Monarchy* from 1867-1914, then to be subject to *Russian Occupation* from 1914-15.

In fact, by the mid-1800s, there were almost 600,000 Jews in the parts of Ukraine under Russian rule. Many more lived in parts of modern Ukraine that then belonged to the above-mentioned *Austro-Hungarian Empire*. The province for that short spell was called the *General-Government Galitsiia*. According to the Russian census in 1897 there were 1,927,268 Jews in Ukrainian regions, accounting for 9.2% of the total population. The pogroms of 1881–1884 were carried out throughout Ukrainian areas.

From 1915-18 the administration of Bolechow reverted to the situation pertaining from 1867-1914, only for the State within which it lay to change from 1918-May 1919 to the *Western Ukrainian Peoples Republic*. However it was during the Civil War and this <u>short period of Ukrainian independence</u> between 1918 and 1920 that the worst pogroms took place since the *Khmelnitsky uprising* in 1648. For, whilst the Jews finally received equal rights with the Ukrainian majority in July 1917, the White (anti-Bolshevik) and Ukrainian nationalist armies, as well as local militias, launched vicious pogroms against the Jews after this, murdering thousands.

May 1919 saw the town of Bolechow becoming part of the *Republic of Poland* and within the *Stanislawow Province* and the *Dolyna district*, and this was to hold until September 1939, when the town became part of the *Ukrainian Soviet Socialist Republic*, and therefore part of the USSR. In June 1941, the town and its region fell under German occupation, being controlled by the *"General Government"* until July 1944. During this Nazi period, close to one million Jews were murdered in Ukraine, notably by the *Einstazgruppen* and <u>local Nazi collaborators</u>. This I understand to mean Ukrainian nationals committing the ultimate betrayal of fellow countrymen, though I am not sure whether Ukrainian Jews were actually seen as fellow countrymen. The most notorious massacre of Jews in Ukraine was to take place at *Babi Yar* just outside Kiev, where 33,771 Jews were killed in a single operation on 29-30 September 1941. I have not been able to establish whether there were any relatives of Michel Halpern who were living in the Ukraine at the time and who were to perish in this way.

In 1944, Bolechow and its region reverted to being under the control of the Soviet Union. Since 1991, it has formed part of the *independent Republic of Ukraine*, and the town of Bolechow is now part of the *Ivano-Frankivs'k oblast*, being a municipality in its own right since 1993.

More significantly for my story, the ethnic make-up of the town remained steady until the 1930s, changing dramatically after the rise to power of Hitler in Germany. For whilst the Jews had formed around three-quarters of the population of 3-4,000, they were obliterated during the period of the Second World War, still registering as zero in 2001, with a mere two Jewish families recorded in the town's population in the early 1990s.

Eastern Galicia, with its 'district capital' L'viv, was, in recent history, famous as being the home for thousands of Jewish people. Yet this group of people was ruthlessly eradicated, with the willing assistance of many local

Ukranians. In his book 'The Lost: A Search for Six of Six Million', Daniel Mendelsohn describes how many of his ancestors lived in Bolechow until the Second World War, when 'the lucky few' made it to safety in the United States. Daniel's grandparents had emigrated to the States around the turn of the nineteenth century, but his family history research had left some gaps which bugged him. More specifically, just as the window of freedom was closing rapidly at the beginning of the Second World War, there was at least one member of his family who elected to stay behind in Bolechow, but Daniel was struggling to establish what happened to several other members last heard of in Bolechow. He travelled to L'viv and Bolechow around 2005, and, with the help of a local genealogist, tried to establish what had happened to his 'missing' ancestors. Furthermore, the *Gesher Galicia* web-site has posted a description of events in Bolechow from around 1941, and I have extracted some of what seem to be the salient events.

The occupation of this part of Eastern Galicia from 1941 was not good news for Bolechow's Jewish population. First there were people exiled to Siberia for not co-operating fully with the Soviet militia, and, when German forces replaced the Soviets, things became even worse. All Jewish businesses were closed and industry was transferred to the German army, bringing further economic hardship. Day-time movement restrictions were put into place and a strict night-time curfew was imposed. Leaving town was forbidden.

Tens of thousands of Trans-Carpathian Jews were said to have been chased across the Carpathian Mountains into Galicia by the Hungarian authorities, and some were moving in a southerly direction, passing through towards Stryj. Others perished in a horrible massacre at Halicz and elsewhere. The Bolechowers helped them greatly by giving them food and clothes. About one hundred of them remained in Bolechow until the very end, as also happened with a number of ex-German Jews. Most of the unfortunates who tried to go back home were murdered in the mountains of the *Skole* frontier. These events deeply shocked the *Bolechowers*.

The former Jewish public school on Szewska Street became the local Judenrat headquarters, from where scores of Jews were sent out to maintain roads, railways, etc., without pay. In the autumn of 1941 all Jews living in nearby villages were forced to move into Bolechow on short notice. They were allowed to take with them only a few belongings. That meant the deportation brought hundreds of deprived people, most of who would soon starve to death.

Working Jews got some wages until December 1942, although the wage was extremely low. Most people had to sell their possessions of every kind. Often these were bartered for food, with a very cheap exchange rate. A new class of `Christian merchant' was born, specializing in the trade of Jewish belongings. Many of these merchants travelled to the agricultural region of Podole in order to sell their ill-gotten haul, then buying food.

From early autumn, dozens of men, women and children, mainly the poor of the town and those expelled, went from door to door begging for food, and most were horribly swollen from hunger. People began eating stinging nettles and the soup served by the *Judenrat*. Mortalities rose from several per day to 40+ in the winter of 1942. By then it was estimated that between six- and eight hundred (Jews) had lost their lives as Jewish police were breaking into dwellings to pull out dead bodies. In stark contrast, some relatively well-to-do Jews still managed to live more or less normal lives, and some were even known to have employed Gentile housemaids as well as providing their children with private lessons.

Both the Ukrainian and Polish press, notably the L'wow *"Gazeta L'wowska,"* was filled with anti-Semitic attacks of the lowest and most venomous kind. The same is true for the many pamphlets, wall posters, etc. in the *"Der Sturmer"* style, often warning of the danger coming from the dirty Jews, spreading typhoid and lice, and advising how to avoid contact with them. It goes without saying that Jews were deeply depressed by the situation. But even after the most horrible news of huge mass executions in L'wow and Stanislawow, some still showed optimism, perhaps as a denial mechanism.

Religious activity was then intense, with prayers held in private houses under tight guard. People were ready to disperse immediately. This was in spite of the prohibition against gathering in groups of more than ten.

During the autumn of 1941, a shortage of food prevailed in Eastern Galicia, owing to floods and plundering by German troops and their allies. This furthered the will of the Germans to hasten the *"Final Solution"* in the region. The mass murder of the Jews began in October, earlier than elsewhere in 'General Government' area in this, the *'Distrikt Galizien'*. Some tried to acquire poison. Later there were attempts of suicide and successful suicides by dozens of Jewish residents, involving whole families. In many cases, poison was ineffective. This continued until the end of the occupation. The Polish population as a whole was rather sympathetic to the Jews of Bolechow, in contrast to L'wow, the "Distrikt" capital. The worst anti-Semitism came from the new class of "*Volksdeutsche*," i.e. people having some ethnic German roots. At dawn on Tuesday, October 28th, several covered trucks arrived from Stanislawow with uniformed SS men and gravediggers with their tools. Ukrainian police and members of the Ukrainian youth organization, "Sitch" from Drohobycz, as well as reinforcements of German police from Stryj, and probably other formations, started arresting Jews beginning at about 10 am. They had lists with hundreds of names of intelligentsia, merchants, rabbis, and so on. The first stage was silent. They took most of the victims by surprise. There were no arrests of women and children until the afternoon. Those people apprehended were instructed to dress well, since they were told that they were embarking on what was to be "a long journey." During the arrests, searches were made in order to loot valuables.

In the next few hours many people on the lists succeeded in hiding and, as a result of this, it was believed, other Jews were indiscriminately caught instead. It appears that both types of "action" were implemented: the "intelligentsia action" (also carried out on the Poles) and the "mass extermination action".

In the afternoon, the description continues, many shots could be heard, along with the commotion caused by the ever-present crowd that was bent on looting. One could see the Jews being dragged out of their hideouts in attics and basements. No one could see or hear how these bands were raiding streets and houses, capturing, beating and extraditing Jews. On the other hand, many Jews found refuge in their [so called] Christian neighbours' houses, often only after agreeing to make large payments or provide expensive presents. But quite often these "trusted friends" chased out the Jews or denounced them after receiving the money or the like. Then they participated in robbing their victims' houses or worse. In general, `Christian' houses were not subject to searches, especially in the first action. As there was a pause as night approached, hiding Jews who were in hiding were able to profit from it. They brought food, warm clothes, etc. In the early morning of Wednesday, October 29th, the intensive searches resumed and continued until noon. The action was stopped at a predetermined time and those caught afterwards were released. At the same time, some 800 – 950 Jews detained in the hall of the former D.K.A. (Red Army House or "Catholic House") were about to begin [what was to be] their last journey, after being subjected to a horrible physical and mental suffering that defied description.

17 ACCOUNTABILITY

The internet and satellites have been the facilitators of an extraordinary revolution in communications. They have permanently changed our perception of the world and of the distance between places on our planet. Thus, whilst cables lying on ocean-beds have allowed us to speak to others on the other side of the globe via the telephone, this can be relatively expensive, thereby limiting its take-up by the world's populace. The world-wide web and the email facility have made instant long-distance communication affordable to many more of us, to the point whereby we can converse via web-cam at a mere fraction of the cost of an international telephone call. And we can see each other into the bargain!

It is rather sad that the red-painted, Gilbert Scott designed, telephone boxes that were such an important public facility in the 1950s have, by and large, been removed from street-corners, and that many of those that remain have been vandalised. We had two phone-boxes, one at either end of the village of Ufford in the 1950s and 1960s, and these provided an essential life-line for the villagers. We did not have a telephone at home, nor did most others in Ufford. The introduction of Subscriber Trunk Dialling [STD] allowed people to be increasingly independent of the [telephone] Operator at the nearest telephone exchange, since even direct long-distance ['trunk'] mainland calls could now be made independently by individuals. Local calls [other than 999 emergency calls] cost 4 [old] pence, and longer-distance calls were priced geographically, as they are today. You pressed button ` A' when the person you were calling answered your call and you wanted to speak to them, or button` B' if there was no response and you wanted any money that you had inserted into the money-box returned to you. The red telephone box near to the Barrack Corner is still there, but now serves as a book-depository for a mobile- library service.

Letter-writing continued to be the accepted means of communication for most people, but I could not have explored my parents' past, especially my mother's, without the internet. My first 'brush' with computers was around 1993, when, as a bachelor studying part-time for a Masters in Construction Management, I had invested in a second-hand IBM 206 slim lined personal computer sold to me by a friend in my block of flats, so that I could word-process my course-work and thesis. For me at the time, IBM was simply the name of an American computer manufacturer with research- and production/sales facilities near Winchester and Portsmouth in Hampshire, UK, and competing with Apple Mac for the personal computer market.

In the mid-1980s, when working as an architect / landscape architect for Richmond [West London] architects Darbourne and Darke, I had undertaken some landscape work-inspection at a new research facility which my firm had designed for IBM next to its existing UK base near Winchester. I had yet to discover the significance of IBM in relation to the firm's earlier engagement by Hitler's régime for the purposes of formulating a comprehensive war-time database of the Jewish inhabitants of Europe. Not that it would have made any difference to my inspection whatsoever!

Here then was IBM in the 1930s and early 1940s, a very large international [main-frame?] computer manufacturer seemingly placing profit before humanitarian considerations. Was it, by the same token, Switzerland's banking activities as a 'neutral' country with an economy largely dependent on its financial sector during the Second World War, that persuaded the high-ranking Swiss member of the Committee of the International Red Cross -based in Geneva - to over-rule other Committee members and lead his organisation to refrain from openly criticising the Nazis' horrific anti-Semitic activities?

It has been said that the Swiss were seen as helping ruthless international capitalists and dictators avoid taxes and protecting their wealth. In World War II, neutral Switzerland appeared to help Nazi Germany financially, while taking deposits from Jewish victims of the Holocaust. It failed to return many of the assets after the war and in recent years some Swiss banks have agreed multi-million pound settlements with families to avoid being sued. Of course, I am conscious that a number of Jewish people resident in the United States have been accused over recent years of exploiting Swiss Banks' wartime greed by themselves being greedy in seeking financial compensation from these banks. Indeed, lawsuits have too often, sadly, become identified with the US. Such criticism, I believe, was inevitable, and could easily have been foreseen to besmirch Jewish people in general. To that extent, the 'opportunistic' efforts were not helpful in relation to the importance of maintaining an unblemished record and memory of the Holocaust. And, anyhow, no amount of money can compensate for the unspeakable acts perpetrated by the Nazis and their collaborators. Yet - and to take Austria as an example with which I am personally familiar - whilst a distinguished international committee was appointed to oversee the distribution of a Nazi victims 'compensation allocation voted-in by its Government, that total sum was but a small token gesture, especially in relation to the large number of verified survivors, relatives of survivors and relatives of victims who sought some kind of restitution. And, for the record, the extent of savings and investments which Austrian Jews held in Austrian banks during WW2 was used as a factor in determining individual payments. Yet, whilst efforts have, for example, been made to return stolen art-pieces to the families of their rightful – but deceased - owners, a very large number of those families' dwellings came to 'made-over' to those Nazis or their sympathisers who were happy to 'sally their hands' with them. Surely this is a case of unconscionable `*expropriation without compensation*' for descendants of that European Jewry who, like my maternal ancestors, were literally driven out of their said homes into the fire and gas of mass extermination. Would the image of carrion crows be too far amiss here?

I would not have known about restitution were it not for the internet. Therefore, I would say in retrospect that one of the most important steps in tracing my maternal ancestors' lives was taken the day that my wife Lynne and I first invested in a personal computer in the mid- 1990s. And, strange though it may seem in today's computer-dependent age, it was used primarily as a word-processor so as to dispense with the need for [even electric] typewriters.

At the time, we would invite overseas students to stay with us to improve their English and visit places near our home in West Yorkshire. All the organising with participating families and student-exchange bodies was carried out by exchanges of letters and phone-calls to intermediaries. Only when we subscribed to wired-internet did we begin to `speak to the world', and this ability became the catalyst for piecing together my family-history and unwrapping a part of my identity hitherto unknown. In an instant, I was able to retrieve data, the existence and relevance of which was appearing before my amazed eyes for the first time ever.

I recalled earlier how my late mother had asked me to dig out old photographs and other documents shortly before she died in late 1991. These were the items that, years earlier, she had kept in her locked-up suitcase in our cottage in Ufford. There were photographs of her brother Hans and of a bygone boyfriend sweetheart who mum had maybe left behind in Vienna, as well as postcards of places she had visited as a young teenager, and photographic mementoes of her travels. Missing, though, was any record of her mother and father, not to mention her grandparents. Mum had long kept an old Austrian passport, but eventually she must have thrown that away. Maybe it was in order to keep memorabilia to a bare minimum, or maybe not?

Intuitively, I had been searching the internet for clues as to my mother's past, entertaining the notion that there was a family-connection with the Holocaust. I was soon to come across a database of Austrian victims, and eventually tracked down an entry for an `Anna Halpern' who had died in 1942. Mum had told me that her mum was called Anna and that I had been named after Anna's husband Michel.

What transpired to be the final seven or so months of mum's life were far from pleasant for her, but she never ceased to remain brave and upbeat, showing no self-pity whatsoever. She had felt sufficiently unwell on the Easter Saturday of 1991 to go across the road from our flat in West London to the doctor's surgery in the adjoining shopping centre. Neither of us had hitherto needed to see a doctor for years, such that when we moved to the flat, mum did not consider it essential that she transfer her GP registration to the doctors' practice near our flat. Consequently, mum was regarded as an `outsider' by the doctors' receptionist that morning and was denied an appointment with one of the doctors that day. Instead, she was given an appointment on the Tuesday following the Easter Monday. Mum duly kept her Tuesday appointment, and the doctor recognised her symptoms and immediately referred her to Charing Cross Hospital, the nearest A &E unit to home. On reflection, I should have intervened on the Saturday and insisted that I accompany my mother straight down to Charing Cross Hospital as soon as the doctors' receptionist refused to grant her an immediate appointment. Whilst it transpired that mum's cancerous growth had spread too far by that Easter, I am still asking the question that re-occurs across the country daily: how well placed are doctors' receptionists to make critical calls like that? With respect, these people do not have a medical background, and I believe that, short of referring every new appointment request to one of the on-duty doctors, surgeries need to employ people who are better able to make judgements, as with call-centre staff on the end of 999 telephone-calls. That said, events in both our lives took a new turn at that point.

Facing inevitable death within months, did mum entertain the thought of telling me about her childhood and early teenage years? I shall never know. Besides, we had too many other things on our minds, and family history was not one of them for me. Pain control and management were foremost considerations as mum began a course of chemotherapy. Mum was not one to tolerate being told half-truths by any consultant oncologist, and was therefore happy that the young Irish house-doctor assigned to her was prepared to be absolutely frank at all stages of her illness. Yet she was insistent that my brother John was not to be informed of her worsening condition, and I can only think that she did not want to burden him unduly, because he was going to have to be told at some point in time.

The first five or so months from diagnosis was a period of regular hospital Oncology Department visits for chemotherapy, allied to outpatient appointments for blood tests and check-ups. Both mum and I were aware that the chemo was purely palliative, alleviating the pain and symptoms without eliminating the actively cancerous growth. But it did give mum some valuable respite from the pain that she had to endure, and when she felt well enough, we took train excursions to places like Cambridge to enjoy the summer sunshine and warmth and pleasant surroundings. I was also able to pop out of the flat for a few hours during the day to join a BT Tec NVQ course at the West London College near Olympia and learn about Information Technology and become proficient in touch-typing, word processing, databases and spreadsheets. I have to admit that I struggled to concentrate fully on what we were being taught and that I returned to the college to complete the course after mum's death.

There came a time when the Chemo treatment was becoming decreasingly effective to the point where it was terminated and mum was left with a combination of pain-killing drugs to take several times a day. By this time, a young lady Spanish doctor had taken over responsibility for mum's 'wellbeing' and it was she who had informed mum about how long she might be expected to live. Mum had been given an open invitation to admit herself into hospital whenever the pain became too much. By the same token, I was allowed to stay as long with her at her hospital-bedside as I wished, irrespective of the stipulations on visiting-hours. I recall how I would go the hospital visitors' cafeteria in the hospital to buy some food for mum, because, even though she was not a pernickety person when it came to food, the patients' meals were not particularly palatable. Most days I would walk down to the hospital from home and this would be a brisk 25 minute journey that would take me through Hammersmith Broadway and passed the new offices of Harper Collins the publishers. Close to her death, and anticipating that the trip mum chose to make from home to the cancer-ward might well be her last, she told me she did not want to die at home because she did not think it was fair on me. I did not mind either option but appreciated her selflessness, though I accepted that, at this stage in her illness, her pain-control medication was probably best administered on the hospital ward.

I had spent the night on the ward on mum's penultimate night, but the following night, with mum's agreement, I went home for some sleep. Sadly, that would become mum's night of passing; I had arrived at the hospital shortly after 6 in the morning, having snatched a few hours of sleep the previous night. Anticipating my early arrival and expecting that I would be heading straight for mum's ward-cubicle, one of the nurses was waiting in the lift-lobby to tell me of mum's death two or hours earlier, and that mum's body had by then be taken to the hospital's Chapel of Rest.

Immediately after mum died, I vowed to inform my brother of the situation, having undertaken the administrative matters which had to be tied up both in the hospital and at the Registry of Births, Marriages and Deaths in the old Fulham Town Hall. I still recall calling in at a local workingmen's café near the old Town Hall for a bite to eat, and coming to terms with a new chapter in my life. I subsequently made my way up to John's 'digs' near Edgeware Road Underground Station in north-west London, to leave a message for him, explaining briefly mum's death and asking him to come round to my flat that evening on his return from work. When John arrived, and with his agreement, we went together down to Charing Cross Hospital so that John could pay his last respects to his mum.

Funerals and cremations were not things that John or I were at all familiar with, besides which, grieving was, especially for me, painful to endure. Whilst I can't speak for John, I possibly had the greater emotional attachment to mum because we had always lived together and I had nursed her at home through her final illness. The cremation service was short, tearful and very private. Whilst mum and I had known several people in the block of flats which had been 'home' to us for thirteen or so years, there were none who counted as true-friends and who might therefore have been invited. John and I had left it to the undertaker to organise the funeral and the officiating minister, and, since John and I had attended an Anglican church many years earlier, they had chosen an Anglican priest. The minister officiating at the cremation service was the minister of the Anglican Church virtually opposite our block of flats in Shepherd's Bush, though I was not to meet him until a few days before the service. He had been asked by our funeral undertaker to officiate at the service. I subsequently attended Sunday morning services at the church for a while after mum's funeral, and whilst I could still remember 'by rote' the liturgy of the regularised church service of my youth, I was left questioning whether this was more important to me as a member of the congregation than listening to God's Word, even at home. I welcomed the whispered chat I was able to have with an elderly church-goer who always sat in the furthest pew from the altar but eventually forsook that in favour of sorting things out in the lonely flat that I had returned to and pondering on my future.

At this point in time I was not even conscious that I was Jewish through mum's line. Mum had consciously chosen our introduction to the Anglican Church when we were young, rather than being incorporated within a Jewish community in Suffolk. Both John and I had subsequently been christened when we were babies. Yet mum had died despite my prayers and this had knocked my faith in God. It would need friends to restore and underpin my faith and answer my questions.

We had all cut off ties with dad by now, though in retrospect I recognise that I was selfish and unthinking not to try to contact him and inform him of mum's death. And neither John nor I had been in touch with Cousin Stan, his wife Anne and other relatives on my dad's side, on Tyneside. It had been more than ten years since mum and I had been in contact with my dad, and much longer for my brother. Sadly, mum's profound distrust of dad had led to their effective separation, though my brother has not fully confided on why he left home in Ufford in 1970, leaving dad on his own, and never to return 'home' during dad's lifetime. Another chapter had thus been opened in both dad's life and that of my brother John, but dad was never to know about what direction mum, John and I had taken in our lives.

What transpired to be the final perusal of family photographs was poignant for both mum and me, though, as I said, her more personal photos only touched her early family history at the edges. There was the photo of her Viennese boyfriend and one or two of her childhood postcards that she had managed to look after since leaving Vienna in 1938. The very request by mum to dig out the photos was for me a coded way of conceding that life on earth for her was finally drawing to a close. One of the last things she asked me to remember, as she lay in her hospital bed, was 'Lest we forget', although we had not discussed her childhood and the Holocaust. Yet I believe she could anticipate that John and I would, sooner rather than later, come face to face with the grim fate that befell her side of the family, and, in confronting the profoundness of the mass destruction of the European Jewry, would come to appreciate the significance of her words.

Mum had taken a number of major steps in her life: leaving her mum and brother at home in Vienna in June 1938 – in full knowledge of the fate that was certain to befall them - in order to save her own life; opting to stay in England and see out the Second World War rather than treating London as a stopping-off point on a longer journey to the United States; further opting to assimilate herself into British society rather than marry into an Anglo-Jewish family; turn her outward back on her Jewish roots and bring up her two boys to at least have some understanding of Christianity; turn her back on a marriage which, arguably, would have been hard to save; and, finally, opting to pull down the shutters on the wider world which she had at one time embraced.

In 1938 about 200,000 Jews lived in Vienna, most of them within a 22 square km radius of the 2nd and 9th Districts. With the invasion of the Nazis, the Jews were suddenly deprived of all their rights, their jobs, their homes, their belongings and their dignity. About two thirds of Austrian Jews were able to emigrate before the borders closed. Those who could not – some 60,000 Jewish men, women and children – were deported to concentration camps principally at Mauthausen, Dachau and Auschwitz, but including Izbica, where mum's mother Anna was to be put to death, and Maly Trostinec, near Minsk, where mum's brother Hans was also a victim of Nazi mass-murders.

Many of the Viennese Jews, who made their way to England whilst they were able, did proceed to travel on to the United States; but a good number did chose to stay and assimilate with the British. But Jewish historian Anthony Grenville, in his book `*The Jews from Germany and Austria in Britain, 1933-1939'*, asserts that those Jews that came to Britain in 1938/39 were not a representative cross-section of the German and Austrian Jewry as a whole. And Mr Grenville believes that the British refugee-community would have been very different if, instead, it was representative. In drawing upon a vast range of testimonies from Viennese and German refugees to make it to London, he says that the Viennese Jews were instead drawn disproportionately from the First-, Eighth- and Ninth-Districts of Vienna; these were the Districts where the Jews were more secularised, assimilated and middle-class in terms of life-style, prosperity and occupation, being well educated and closely associated with the German speaking culture of the city to which they had contributed so much. Yet the largest concentration of Jews in Vienna had lived in the *Leopoldstadt* or *Mazesinsel*, Vienna's Second District, where, in Mr Grenville's view, the Jews tended to be poorer, working class, Orthodox and closer to the traditional lifestyle and customs of Eastern Europe. That said, mum had lived with her mother and brother in the said *Leopoldstadt* area, and in the short street called *Pillersdorfgasse*, to be precise. Yet, I would have suggested that mum was middle-class and as educated as one could expect from a nineteen year old young lady who had been forced to make a quick and final exit from her family and her homeland, for fear of her own life. Mr Grenville, in this respect, accepts G.S. Troller's report-conclusion that the fate of many of the `oberservant'/orthodox Hassidic Jews from the Leopoldstadt was Auschwitz, whereas the middle-class, cultured Jews managed [at the Austrian end] to overcome the obstacles to emigration in the short period of time between the **Anschluss** and the outbreak of war. Anyhow, my perception of` middle-class' - shaped by my upbringing and later life - may not necessarily match the Austrians' perception of that `class'. The difference between mum and many of the other Viennese refugees was that, unmarried, she had already given birth to John in 1943, that she had married our dad Harold in 1944, that I was born a week after the end of the War and that our parents opted to start a new life in rural Suffolk. So whilst, according to records accessed by a member of staff at the London-based Association of Jewish Refugees, mum had evidently attended their north London social events after she had arrived in London from the early summer of 1938, any new Jewish links that she may have formed were now being left behind for good in north London, and by choice. In short, mum had opted for assimilation.

In my earlier e-mail exchanges with Georg Spitaler at DÖW in Vienna, more than ten years ago, Georg had at one point suggested that mum's family had not always lived at Pillersdorfgasse, in Vienna's Second District, but had been moved there from another part of the city by the Nazis, possibly as a move preparatory to the final liquidation of these Jews. I did not pursue this line of thought at the time and have yet to verify the situation for myself. He also suggested at one point that mum's dad Michel Halpern had ancestors who had been important members of the Jewish faith community, and, in this respect, he might have been referring to life in Bolechow in Eastern Galicia/Ukraine. I hope to be able to clarify this by the time that the sequel to this book is being written.

So what would mum's dad Michel have made of the goings-on in his former homeland of western Ukraine in the last few decades ..... or indeed these last few months of 2014/15? Given that mum was only about three years old when her father died, I guess that `grown-up' conversation she may have had about his homeland would have been when she a bit older, and, even then, with her mother. Her dad had become unwell when she was a mere toddler and it was more than enough that her mum Anna was trying to cope with Michel's failing health as well as trying to run the home and bring up their two children on what must have been on a tight budget. That said, I did not discover where Michel was born or who his parents were until years after mum died.

18 DARKNESS, TRANSPARENCY, SWINGS AND BALANCES

ong before the *Glasnost* in the former *Soviet Union* attributed to Michail Gorbachev at the end of the 1980s, the departure of thousands of Jews, Germans and Armenians from the USSR to Israel and elsewhere was well known internationally. The deep-felt bitterness felt by the Russians as a result of the huge-scale atrocities inflicted by the Nazis on Russian troops and civilians during the Second World War, is well documented, as are the more recent uprisings of the Armenian Nationalists seeking independence from the` *Soviet Union as was'*. Yet the emigration of 248,900 Jews from the USSR during the period 1971-80 accounted for more than 77% of the total of all Jewish /German / Armenians who left during that period. Why? And how many of these came from the former Soviet Republic of the Ukraine?

Ironically, there had earlier been an influx of Jews into the Ukraine. Stalin's *resettlement policy* of the 1920s-30s [the creation of Jewish agricultural settlements (*kolkhozy)*] brought over 70,000 Jews to Ukraine from the territory of the USSR, primarily Belarus. Secondly, after the disintegration of Poland in 1939 and the annexation of Western Ukraine by Germany, the Jewish population of Ukraine reached just over 1.5 million, or the equivalent of three per cent of the total population of Ukraine. However, during the Second World War, about one-third of the total Jewish population of Ukraine (or 350,000 to 500,000 people) was evacuated, and close to one million Ukrainian Jews were murdered by the Nazis.

There were further post-war population shifts in the USSR, caused firstly by the widespread reluctance of Holocaust survivors to return to their home towns for fear of a hostile reception from the new residents in their abandoned properties; and secondly by the repatriation of about 40,000 former Polish citizens, with Jews making up a significant proportion of these. **Especially significant for this account is the fact that the common thread running through all these mass-migrations of Jewish people is the absence of any sign of integration.**

I fast-forward now to Tuesday, 27th January, 2015. This was the 70th anniversary of the day that the few survivors of the Auschwitz concentration camp were freed and given some` vegetable soup' by the liberating Russian soldiers. Among the people who were interviewed for a British TV programme that day a few weeks back, was Eva Schloss, who, like mum, was a Viennese Jewess. Mum made it to England as a young lady, but, in retrospect, she was lucky. The young Eva Schloss and her family were taken to Auschwitz, although not all survived. Eva's step-father was the father of Anna Frank, who was fatally betrayed whilst in hiding in Holland. As Eva said in her TV conversation that was recorded just before that late January 2015 programme, **we must never forget what happened. And those were among mum's last words to me.** As Eva said, there will be those who continue to maintain that the Holocaust is a fabrication, but we as the offspring of the sufferers, whilst saddened by such aberrations, are nevertheless acutely aware of the importance of remaining vigilant and alert to the dangers that continue to plague Europe and the rest of the world.

My wife and I are re-reading Tom Wright's *Acts (of the Apostles) for Everyone*, Part 1. Dr. Wright, one-time Bishop of Durham and a leading Christian writer on the New Testament of the Bible, describes how, when he had visited Israel to write a book about Christ, he was struggling to write a few vital pages concerning the battles Jesus had over **exorcisms**:

the battles, that is, both with the **demons themselves** and with the people who were accusing Christ of being, himself, in league with the **devil**. Having frustratingly been forced to re-write that particularly difficult section of the book - which had now been lost from his computer after a workman had driven a nail through the electricity supply in his temporary Jerusalem office - Dr. Wright prays that he can speak God's word with all boldness, because he recognises that there is a battle going on in `the heavenlies'; a battle such as Christ had with the sly Jewish religious` leaders' in the Jerusalem Temple in the run-up to the Crucifixion.   Sometimes, Dr. Wright suggests, the battle is with the spirit of the age. Today as then, Christians across the world filled with God's true spirit are battling against those worshipping the spirit of the devil, masquerading as God's spirit. It is not surprising that for this very reason, Christians in Asia, Africa and beyond are persecuted even to death. In being hell-bent on having Jesus killed, the Jewish religious leaders —despite all the signs telling them otherwise - were obstinately in denial that the King whom Jews had waited many centuries for, had actually arrived in the shape of the Jesus that they persecuted, and they had instead succumbed to `worshipping' pagan gods and the dark forces associated with them. Dr. Wright's Christian perspective is that although the battle will not always be with actual dark powers, this latter type of battle cannot be ruled out in the struggle to set people free across the whole world.

Where were/are the swings and balances in Christ's time, during WW2 and today? **Who and what were/are the forces of evil during each of these eras?** Readers must of course judge for themselves!

We have recently seen Jewish shoppers and their families in France murdered by terrorists claiming to be representing Islam. And people from the east of the Ukraine continue to flee to western Ukraine in the face of military aggression by `separatists', allegedly with the support of neighbouring Russia, who are said to want Eastern Ukraine to be annexed to it. Readers of my generation and earlier will recall that, after Turkey invaded Cyprus, the United Nations Security Council installed its peace-keeping force to uphold the `balances' side of the equation on that island, but we have yet to see that in the Ukraine – not to say in present-day Syria and elsewhere - and whilst I am not cognisant of present-day Russia's contribution to the UN coffers, I know that, during the Cold War era, the USSR fell behind in its financial contributions, resulting [at least in part] in a peace-keeping organisation that could only be partially effective at best.

Thus, when commenting recently on the economic sanctions imposed on Russia by the EEC and the US as a consequence of the Ukrainian fighting, a British television commentator remarked that the Russian President was continuing to enjoy extensive support from the Russian population despite – or maybe because of -the worsening state of his country's economy. The commentator believed that it was nationalist pride that underpinned this support. So is it the same pride that seemingly perpetuates the Anti-Semitism emerging/re-emerging in Eastern Ukraine? Unfortunately, and as a case in point, we do not hear a great deal about what ordinary Russians think from across that palpable divide between Russia and its European neighbours.

According to an article in the British *Daily Mail* newspaper in mid-April, 2014, `*In a chilling echo of the Holocaust, Jews are 'ordered to register and list property' in east Ukraine after pro-Russian militants take over government buildings. *'Jews have reportedly been told to register with pro-Russian forces in the east Ukrainian city of Donetsk or face deportation. A pamphlet handed out in Donetsk orders 'citizens of Jewish nationality' over the age of 16 to pay $50 to register and be issued special passports 'marking the confession of faith'. The leaflets, a chilling echo of Nazi persecution, were handed out to Jews leaving a local synagogue by three men in ski masks holding the flag of the Russian Federation, Israeli media reports.'*

This has ominous pointers to the forced inclusion of Israel or Sara in your name for identification purposes – as happened to my mother's mother and brother - so the `signs' are worrying for outsiders in Western Europe, though obviously more-so for the target-peoples in the Ukraine and European Jews in general. However, none of us can afford to be complacent, as witness the murder of Jews at a French supermarket at the time of the *Charlie Hebdo* massacre in Paris in early 2015, and the reporting of events. The group *Reporters Sans Frontières* [**Reporters Without Borders**] condemned what it called the "presence of 'predators'" in a protest-march over the *Charlie Hebdo* massacre. The group said it was "appalled by the presence of leaders from countries where journalists and bloggers are systematically persecuted" such as Egypt, Russia, Turkey and the United Arab Emirates.

Thus, in describing how `generic extremist groups and totalitarian regimes' committed large-scale crimes in recent European history - as a corollary to recounting my family's journey – I hasten to reassure readers that I have not been lulled for one minute into believing that the United Kingdom has some kind of idyllic democracy that should serve as a model for other states to follow. Indeed, totally unacceptable behaviour can be more subtle in the UK.

The miscarriages of justice linked to the perceived unwillingness of the judiciary and their medical `Gurus', the ` Medical Establishment', to seriously entertain breakthroughs in medical research, are mere examples of serious failings by the all-powerful `Greater Establishment.' I have come across one instance whereby a qualified medical practitioner, working as a university medical researcher, was struck off the UK's General Medical Council [GMC] register for deigning to hold – with good reason - that certain inherited disorders could account for symptoms that hitherto led unerringly, but rightly or wrongly, to court-rulings such as grievous bodily harm. The fact that the availability of legal aid has been drastically reduced and that so-called `Defence counsel' can in a number of such cases be made up of under-motivated government-financed `duty-barristers'- suggests that at the outset, the odds could be stacked against potentially innocent defendants. The likelihood that the prosecution [Crown Prosecution Service alongside local authority organisations] and their aggressive barrister-counsel are known, on occasion, to have been determined to ride rough-shod over due-process to achieve a `successful' prosecution, needs no further comment from me than to state that it is a flagrant abuse of human rights. In a related vein, the Family Courts in England, as I write in early 2015, still operate under a veil of secrecy despite the British newspaper *Daily Mail's* proclamation in January 2014 that this was about to change. The paper's headline announced

"At last! Victory on secret courts: Rulings in family cases to be made public after Mail campaign"

Yet, more than a year on, things have not changed, with children still being kept in care despite the accused parents being exonerated in the courts. And newspapers and TV are not allowed to acquire and then report case-information because, in so doing, they would still be contravening the reporting-restrictions laws that are imposed by the Family/Children's Courts. This means that neither the affected families nor society as a whole is able to establish conclusively whether or not `**due process'** has been operative, and whether **miscarriages of justice** have in fact been carried out in secret. A *Channel 4 News* item tonight confirmed this secrecy is still operative. And, furthermore, the public is none the wiser as to *who* or *what* is causing this delay in implementing the desperately needed reporting reforms. So why is this veil of secrecy being perpetuated, and why isn't the Home Secretary being obliged to provide a truthful explanation in the House of Commons or at an All Party Parliamentary Select Committee that deals with family law? And, is it any wonder that some couples, fearing wrongful arrest and prosecution, have fled from the UK with their child/children to avoid what might well turn out to be wrongful imprisonment or unwarranted separation between parents and their children? I am not a medical expert, but I am aware that pharmaceutical companies, with the implicit support of the Medical Establishment, have benefited a great deal financially as a result of statins being dispensed so widely and frequently via Britain's National Health Service; Joe Public has been encouraged to believe that statins `reduce cholesterol', and so *ipso facto* must be good. Yet today – and `after the event' for many patients - it is belatedly acknowledged that certain good cholesterols are important to healthy living and that the taking of statins can, amongst other things, increase the risk of the onset of dementia.

The intentional destruction of vital evidence by officers within police forces, as illustrated by the Stephen Lawrence case and the cover-ups relating to the Hillsborough football stadium tragedy in South Yorkshire, are other examples of `due-process' being blocked for the sake of preventing the failings/inadequacies of officials/professionals from being exposed. Even as I write, the Chief Superintendent Police Officer responsible for policing the FA Cup soccer match so many years ago has, when called to answer questions at a belated inquest into the 96 deaths, confessed that he lied to a match official and that he had personally given instructions for his subordinate officers to open exit-gates to allow thousands of waiting fans to pack into the soccer ground and onto the terraces. This influx of people was the reason why the fans were crushed to death. Yet up till now, the relatives of the dead have not been able to bring closure. But at what cost to them?

Stephen Lawrence, a black British teenager, was murdered in South East London on 22nd April 1993, aged 18. It was suggested in an early court hearing into Stephen's murder that it was racially motivated, that he was killed because he was black, and that the handling of the case by the police and the Crown Prosecution Service [CPS] was affected by issues of race. The marathon fight that Stephen's parents put up to achieve justice for their dead son, led to the breakup of their marriage and unbelievable pain on their part. The parents also wanted to see an end to the endemic racist culture residing in the police force and, seemingly, in the CPS. Eventually, in 2012, and nearly twenty years after the murder, Stephen's killers were convicted and imprisoned, but at what cost to his parents? And whilst a partial revocation of double jeopardy laws allowed the murderers to be brought to justice, time will tell whether the case has brought about profound changes to cultural attitudes on racism within the police forces and other arms of the law in Britain.

Another culture, residing this time in Britain's National Health Service, is the 'character-assassination' of whistle-blowers who dare speak out about wrong-doing, with the protection of these whistle-blowers still no more effective in 2015 than ten years and more earlier. Despite measures introduced by the UK Government to encourage 'safe whistle-blowing', potential new whistle-blowers are now being advised by victimised whistle-blowers not to reveal wrong-doing in the workplace for fear that they too will have their lives destroyed for the sake of protecting hospital patients, whilst the guilty workplace colleagues, operating as a secretive and mutually supportive clique, strive to perpetuate this practice with impunity. There must be countless other instances of a similar nature across the whole spectrum of society's activities, including key influential positions in newspapers' and broadcasters' editorial ranks. Consider, for instance, the case of the political correspondent who recently parted company with his 'right of centre' national daily in the UK because, in his professional work, he claimed that he was unable to freely discuss the rôle of a major international bank – and one of Britain's bigger banks - in relation to alleged tax-avoidance activities by clients of its Swiss private-banking arm. It was claimed that in a situation where there was a possible conflict of interest between the interests of its advertisers –including the said bank – and reporting which might be seen as criticising them, then the advertisers' interests took priority. In denying this claim, the newspaper-proprietor stated that the barrier between journalism and advertising had not been breached. Readers must judge!

I remember becoming a Member of the Royal Institute of British Architects [RIBA] years ago, and even then there was a lively debate inside and outside the Council of the RIBA about whether or not Members wishing to put their names forward for election to Council should be allowed to if they belonged to what were essentially secret societies.

Decades later, and well after the prosecution of John Poulson and architect William Brown , the matter still rumbles on within and without the corridors of power at the RIBA, even though, as a retired architect, I have long since resigned from the said Institute. Nevertheless, it might not be widely known among Brits as a whole that UK architects are obliged to register with the **Architects' Registration Board of the UK** [ARB] in order to call themselves architects and practice as such. Neither might they be aware that it is the ARB that was set up by Parliament as the UK's regulator of architects, and thus to be an independent public interest body with a strong consumer protection rôle. I am at a loss to understand how professionals in the medical and design/engineering sectors - as well as Civil Servants, local authority employees, officers of police forces, etc., etc. – can honestly reconcile compliance with the statutory purposes of their governing bodies and the duty of care that they owe to the general public with submission to complete silence and secrecy demanded by `Secret Societies', serving only the personal interests of its members and over-riding the law in all its facets.

I remember how, following mum's death, I had agreed to run for election as a member of the Lessees' Management Company's Board for the block of flats of which one was mine. Subsequently elected as a Director by the lessees, I began attending meetings with the other three Board Members. I had no unwritten agendas, and as I saw it, the purpose of the said Company was to oversee the management of the overall building and its surrounding land by a firm of estate agents who had been carrying out this work `on the lessees' behalf' for years. We therefore had to make decisions about the expenditure of the considerable service-charge monies which had been collected from the fifty or so lessees every six months, including ensuring that any maintenance- and repair-work to the common-parts was up to standard. There was a good deal of disquiet at the time about the performance of the managing agents, the poor performance of the cleaners, the fact that external decoration of the windows to the flats [extending up five-floors and reached only by scaffold] had been left for so long that the wooden frames had rotted beyond redemption; and the fact that, because repairs to the asphalt flat roof to the whole building had been overlooked for years, the lessees were now being confronted with (inflated) estimates to replace the asphalt and the rotten hardwood window frames.

As a lessee who had questioned the decisions of the managing agents on several occasions during the years that I lived in the block of flats, I was acutely aware of the uncomfortably cosy relationship between my other Board members, the managing agents and the freehold owner, and the fact that lessees were being confronted by disproportionate and rapidly increasing service charges. During the whole of the time that I was on the said Board, I requested documentation relating to a range of issues being raised by the lessees, but on each occasion, my request was being rebuffed. Should I ever have wondered why?....

There came a point whereby there was no point in continuing to represent the lessees on the Board, and so I reluctantly resigned. I was on the `black-list' of those in control, period!

My brief spell as an unpaid Director of the management company had confirmed my suspicions, and, since mum had now died, there was no reason whatsoever for continuing to live there in the longer term. I was soon to move north to `pastures new' to begin a new chapter in my life, and intend to expand on this in the sequel to this book.

What I can say in retrospect is that another of the Board Members was, by his own admission a member of –let's just say - a `secret society'. And, because I was on Christian-name terms with the person, I was' bitterly disappointed by this person's collaboration with the other erring Board Members. Indeed, after I stepped down from the Board, one of the lessees was so disgusted by the poor maintenance that she refused to pay her service charge. My friends and I did try to warn her of the folly of her intended action, but she was determined to go ahead, and this ultimately proved to be costly for her. In not paying that charge in the first instance, she was in breach of her leasehold obligations, and her flat was subsequently re-possessed – and one of my former colleague-directors was able to buy the flat from the Freeholder or mortgagor, and allegedly at a significantly reduced price, and then sell it on for a worthwhile profit. It is a well-known fact that mortgage lenders are keen to dispose of property that they find themselves with as a result of [supposedly] defaulting mortgagees, even at a price somewhat lower than its market price in normal selling conditions. And the difference between the selling price and the amount owed to the lender [i.e., the `negative equity sum'] is a loss which the defaulting lessee has to bear. And many lessees of blocks of flats in other parts of West London, including Earls Court and Kensington, were also long-suffering protesters who I came to meet prior to serving on the Board. I hasten to point out that part of the reason that lessees suffered so much was that the legislation protecting their rights was woefully inadequate and there was reluctance by politicians in power to address this issue. Is it surprising that my admittedly rhetorical question is again `Why?'

Where were – and, indeed, where are - the swings and balances in all these and many more similar situations? Sadly, I have yet to be convinced that we have a transparent democracy whereby our politicians and public servants are truly obliged to be answerable to the electorate. Neither am I persuaded that, as a corollary, there is always an electoral mandate for some important and far-reaching legislation that is being steam-rollered through Parliament by successive governments in power. So should we be surprised at the level of disenchantment surrounding domestic politics which is reflected in low turn-outs at both national- and local-elections?

Control is often abused and rarely shared willingly. Our big challenge is to introduce measures which begin to restore integrity into the public realm, bringing about true answerability and simultaneously arrest this disenchantment. The National Audit Office and the OFSTED schools-and-social services watchdog are valuable – even if blunt and uncoordinated - `instruments' in this respect, but we still do not seem to have any independent body, answerable only to the electorate, which can keep an eye on the performance [and value for money] of the many other aspects of central- and local government that are being rolled out on a daily basis and funded by tax-payers' money. Charity-donors wish to be assured that their contributions are being spent wisely by these charities, so why shouldn't we expect the same demonstrable performance from central- and local government?

Irrespective of our country of origin or ethnicity, our education or our wealth, we are all mere mortals, imperfect, sinful and susceptible humans, liable to be swayed by half-truths and mistruths employed by politicians [used in its widest sense] for the sake of gaining/ holding onto power. Recent European history has demonstrated the extreme outworking of that particular truism at enormous cost. The political cost of relinquishing/delegating true power to the electorate in the UK, of bettering rather than perpetuating the *status quo*, seems presently to be too great in political and financial terms for it to be contemplated by those parties in power and those in opposition, and, as the case may be, their financial backers. We therefore have to remain vigilant in the meantime, whilst pursuing truly democratic ideals and protecting those discriminated against, the vulnerable and the less fortunate in society. I recall reading about the legacy of the war-time destruction of Berlin, a vast area of rubble subsequently left untouched for decades due to the construction of the Berlin Wall and the consequent isolation of East Berlin and East Germany. During that time, Mother Nature was allowed to ` heal' man's destruction, and the result was the emergence of a huge expanse of self-seeded woodland and wildlife, unfettered by man. There is a poignant symbolism about this. In striving to bring the aforementioned aspiration closer to fruition, and so minimize the risk of a recurrence of these events, **we who subscribe to this goal must stand firm in resisting the future erosion of the human rights which ultimately underpin any true democracy**. I, for one, owe it to my late parents to do this.

Child Of The Diaspora

Top photo: Church Lane, Ufford. The Almshouses are to the right foreground, beyond which is the pink house where the Pendles lived when we were young. An RAF officer rented the property during the Cold War, and Jane Woodhouse, my brother John's peer at Ufford Primary School, lived there later. We lived to the left, off the photo.

2nd and 3rd photos: our rented cottage at the time we lived in it. Note the glazing pattern of the dormer casement window, and of the downstairs sliding sash living room window. Note also the open porch with its oak post supports, and how the small clay tiles on the dormer roof curve round to tie-in with the larger clay pantiles of the main roof. Evidently, the roof to this C.16 / C.17 timber-framed cottage was probably thatched originally, like some of the neighbouring cottages in the lane.

4th photo: this became the Hurst family's house a good few years after we first came to Ufford. The Hursts ran an antiques shop in Woodbridge for some years, and mum used to clean the house for the family. This was convenient for mum because all she had to do was walk along the path that ran alongside our part of the allotment and came out onto Barrack Lane just to the right, off the photo.

Child Of The Diaspora

Our former rented cottage, as it is today. The brick chimney stack to our neighbour's side of what are now Lady Cottages, was removed by Gordon E., the owner of the two cottages in the later 1960s, prior to their being listed Grade 2. The simple, open and tiled porch has been replaced and the leaded valley -gutters to the dormer windows have replaced the small plain tiles which once turned the corner between the porch roof and the main roof.

A brick-walled extension has been added to the end of what was our neighbour Ted Taylor's home, presumably to house the new bathroom.

St Mary's Church lies beyond the back garden to what was the Jenveys' cottage. Our shared water-well with its circular base wall and pitched roof was to the left off this photo.

Child Of The Diaspora

The former post office in Lower Ufford, run [during our childhood] by George Evans and his wife. George delivered the post around lower Ufford first thing in the morning. When Mrs Evans became unwell, Bill Walker and his wife took over.

The row of cottages opposite the Lion Inn, where the Kings and the Murphys lived. During the severe flooding of the river, especially in 1953, the water reached the cottages at the far end of the terrace.

Ruby Herndon's former house, where School Lane met the former A12 main road running left to right. School Lane has now been diverted. I don't recollect the hedge across Herndons' garden, and in his poem *Mending Wall,* Robert Frost asks if fences make good neighbours.

Gardeners Cottages in Lower Road, Ufford, where the Millers and the Taylors lived. I think there used to be a shared path on the line dividing the properties, with the Millers' large vegetable garden to the left and Taylors' to the right.

Child Of The Diaspora

Council houses [at least originally!] fronting onto the former A12 main road just before it became the original bypass. I think that Greta Hines and her family lived in one of these houses in the 1950s.

The Lion pub in lower Ufford, where Mr Chilvers was the publican in my childhood and youth. The Chilvers family have been well-known roof-thatchers in East Suffolk for years, using special local long—stemmed wheat..

The former Ufford Football Club pitch, which was rented from a local farmer. In the summer, the field was cut for hay. The players changed at the Lion pub, some 300 or so metres up the road.

The bridge over the River Deben, next to the former soccer pitch. We tended not to swim here because there was greater water-depth further along the river. The meadow in the background is part of the flood-plain, and the river was dredged regularly to control flooding.

Child Of The Diaspora

Dad pictured [middle row,3rd from right] with his fellow troops from the Middlesex Regiment during World War Two. It is said that they were under the command of David Niven at some stage. David was to become famous for his film-roles later in his life.

Mum with my older brother John and myself, probably in later 1946. Mum would have taken us on walks along Spring Lane and out into the peaceful countryside surrounding Ufford, and might have done some cleaning locally to boost family income then.

Child Of The Diaspora

Top picture: Sunday School trip to Campsea Ash to watch cricket. Roy Taylor, my brother and Michael Miller are also in the picture.

2nd picture: John and I hitch-hiking with mum in N. Wales in 1957.

3rd picture: Me seated on my brother's racing bike, on the allotment, around 1958.

4th picture: Me working on our part of the allotment in about 1962. Mrs Barker's cottage is in the background. The holly tree at the end of our shared path to Church Lane, was always the source of our Christmas decorations holly-and-holly-berry sprigs, but has now gone. Residents have prevented the allotment from being built-upon.

5th picture: Me in the back row of the Civic College's Minors League soccer team, circa 1963. 'Jinx' [Bohdan Jelinski, our star striker] is in the bottom row, middle, and John Ablitt is in the bottom-row left, next to our team-manager Stan. Paul Hayward is our goalkeeper.

Child Of The Diaspora

Mum and her brother Hans in 1930. Mum was around 11 years old at the time, and Hans was about 16.

Mum's own mother Anna was now looking after her two children single-handed, and on a widow's pension, because her husband Michel had died some 8 or so years earlier.

The year is 2001, and my brother John is seen here standing outside the front-door to the block of flats in Pillersdorfgasse, in Vienna's 2nd district., being where mum, her brother and their parents lived over different lengths of time, and which mum left in the early summer of 1938 to come to England. There is no name on the door –bell for the flat that mum's parents rented or leased. I later contacted the owner of a shop at the corner of this block of flats, who gave me the occupant's name. But our friend Lisa was unable to elicit any answers to the questions she asked him re: owners when calling shortly after.

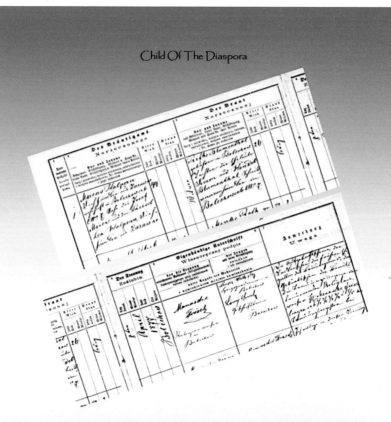

Record of marriage between Marcus Halpern [aged 44] and Rifke Blumenthal [aged 26], which took place on 8th April, 1877 and which records the marriage-witnesses as living in Bolechow, in what was Eastern Galicia and is now the western part of the Ukraine.

My mum's father's was Michel Halpern, who was born in Bolechow in January, 1877, and whilst his birth certificate records his father as being Marcus and his mother as being Rebeka Blumenthal, I believe that the name Rifke can be a more familiar form of Rebeka. On this basis, I am confident that the named couple are my maternal great-grand-parents. Markus's parents are listed as Joseph Maier and Reisel Lea Halpern, whilst Rifke's are recorded as Simon and Heindel Blumenthal.

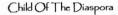

Sketch map of part of Europe in 1940, to give readers an idea of the relative location of places pertinent to the lives of my mother's side of my family.

The concentration camp at Maly Trostinec, where mum's brother Hans was deported to his death, was fairly close to Minsk, which can be seen near the top right-hand corner of the map.

Mum's mother Anna was deported to her death at Izbica, which, to give it its fuller name, was Izbica Kujawska, and was fairly close to Sobibor, which in turn is to the south-west of Minsk. Minsk is now within the state of Belarus.

ABOUT THE AUTHOR

I grew up in a poor-family in a relatively poor but yet socially coherent village community set in the heart of agricultural Suffolk of the 1940s, 50s and 60s.I was extremely privileged at the time in having been allowed to continue my education into sitting my GCEs and A-levels, and then being allowed to embark on full-time training as an architect.

After a number of years working as an architect, I opted to extend my competence by training as a landscape architect, though, unconventionally, whilst working in horticulture and landscape construction management.

I was subsequently to work as both an architect and landscape architect in both private-practice and in local-government, and to extend my skills into the realms of building-conservation and construction-management. Later, I was lucky enough to teach architectural- and building conservation students at my local university in Yorkshire and to teach landscape management at a higher-educational college in North Yorkshire.

My wife Lynne has a nursing- and medical research and teaching-background and together we founded, and are Trustees of a registered charity focussing on supporting families caring at home for relatives who have an acquired or inherited brain injury.